Art Therapy Mandalas

Copyright: Published in the United States by Peter Raymond
Published August 2018
ISBN-13: 978-1724869753
ISBN-10: 1724869752

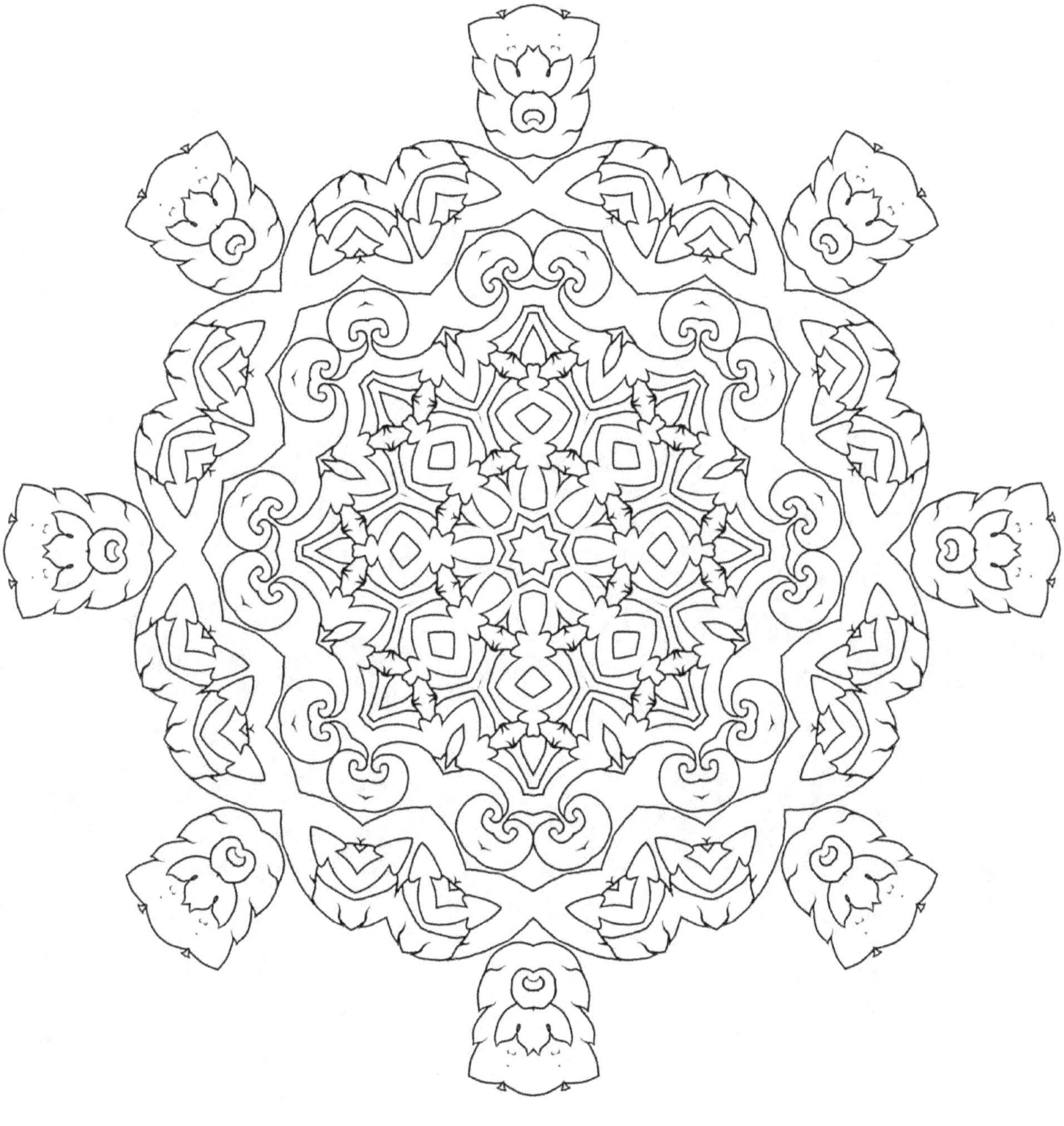

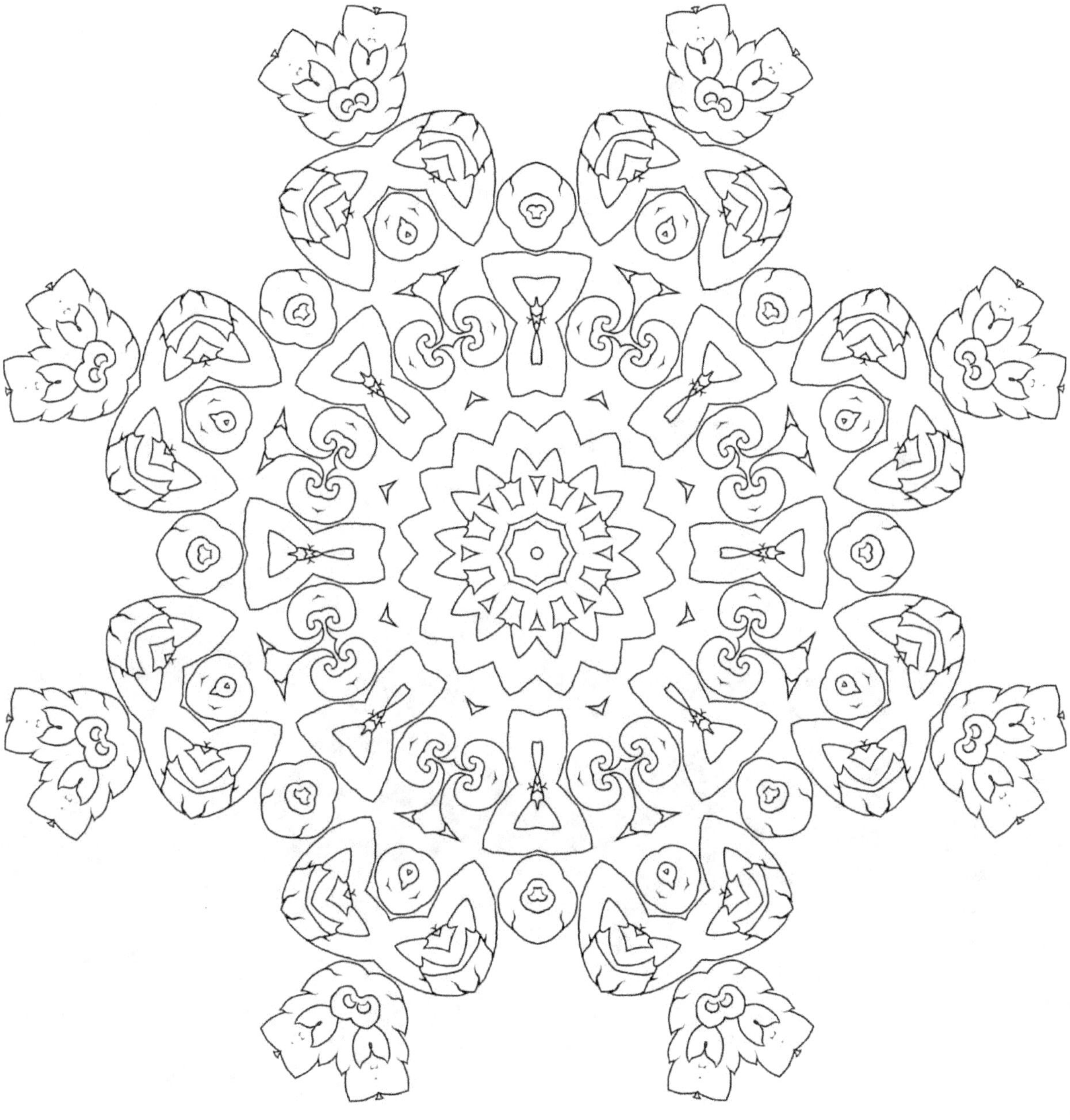

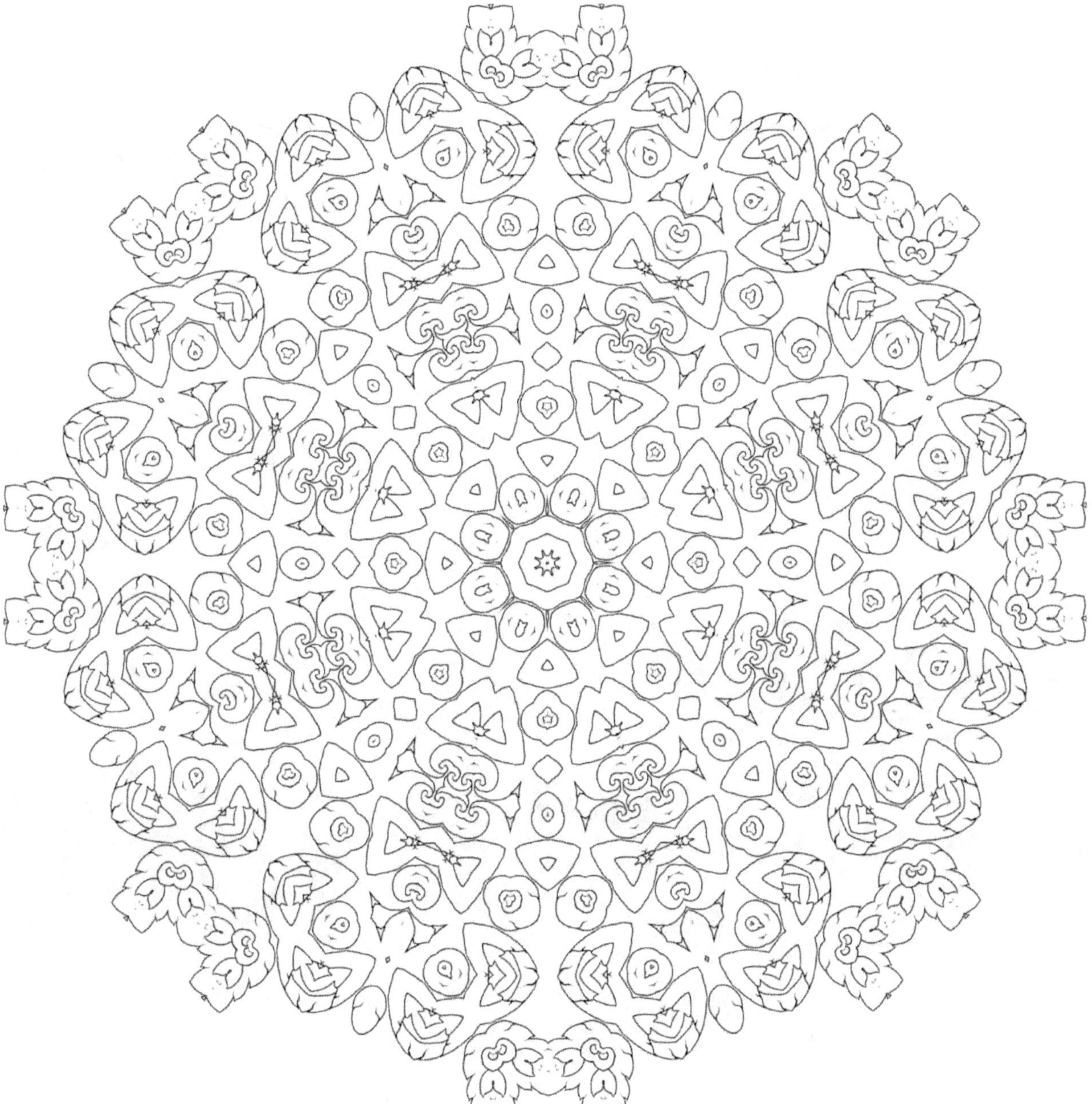

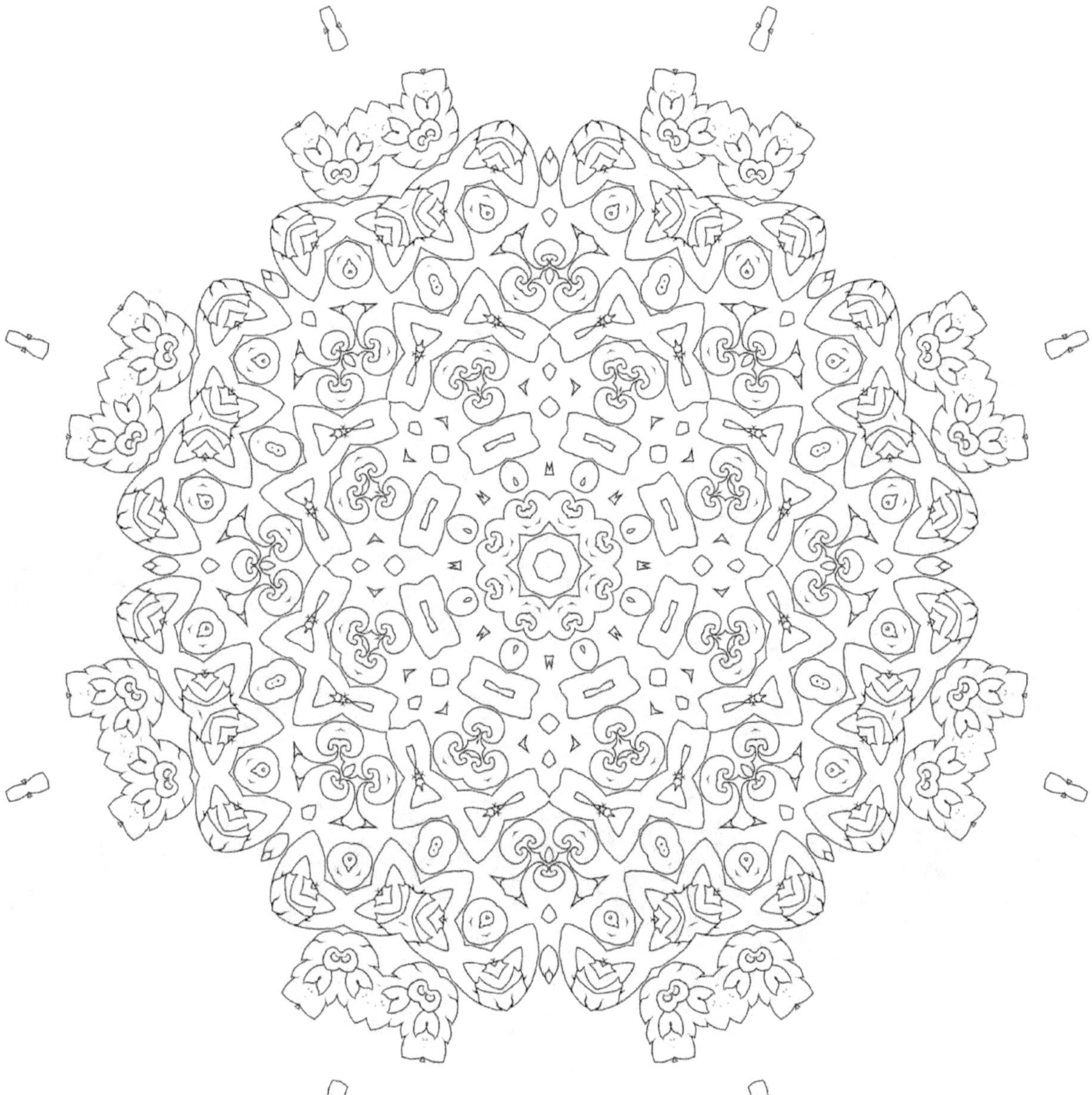

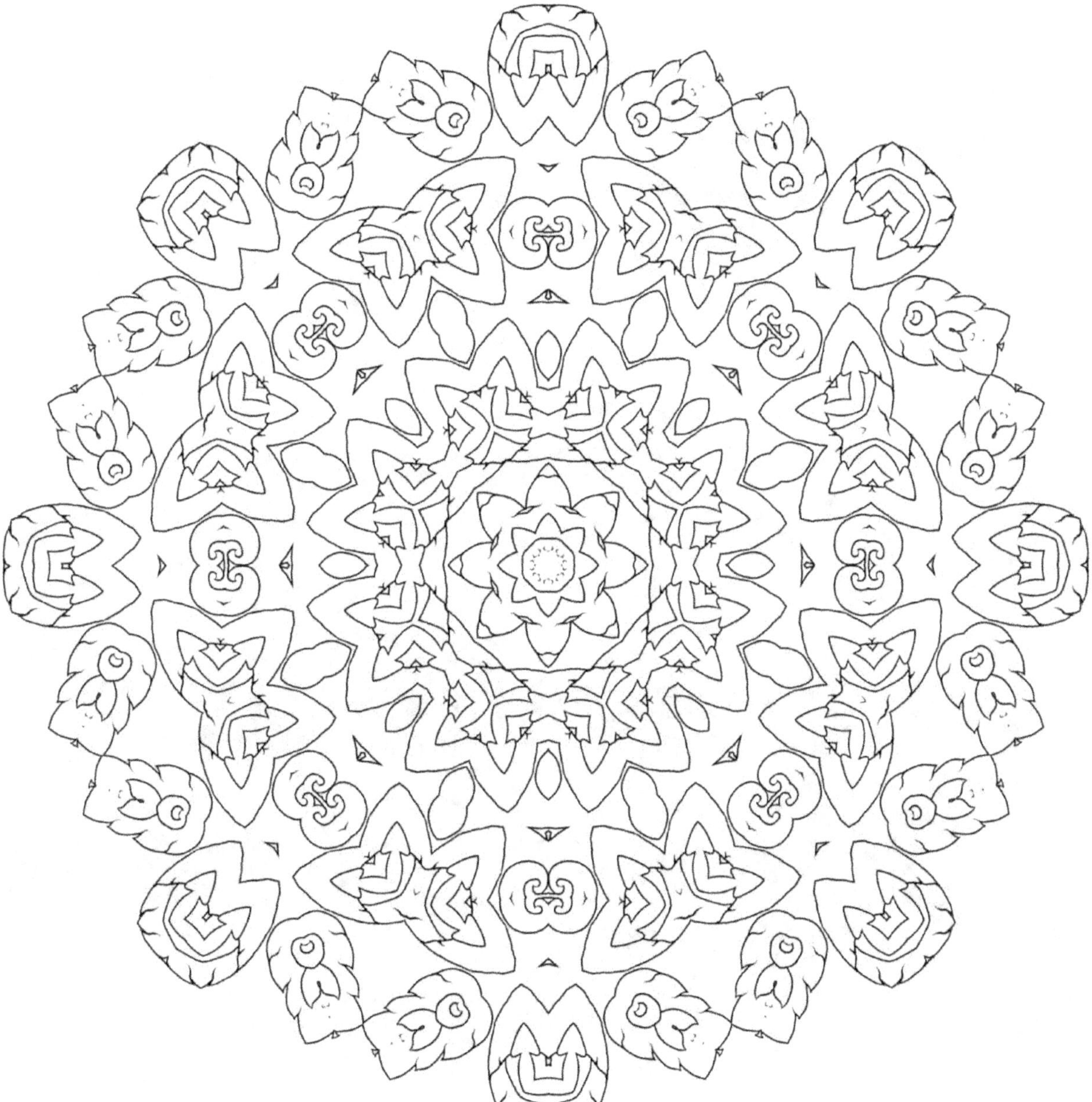

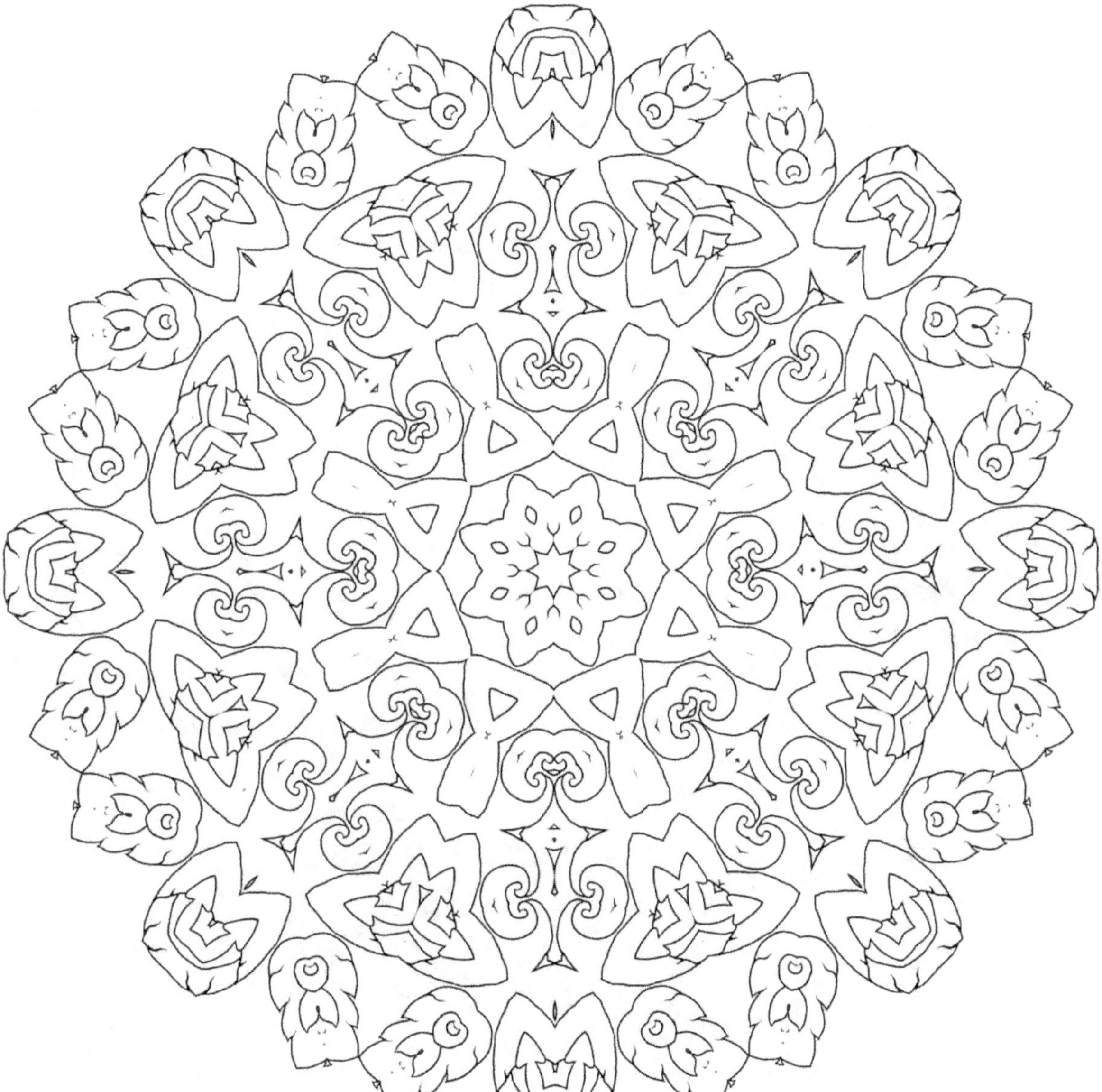

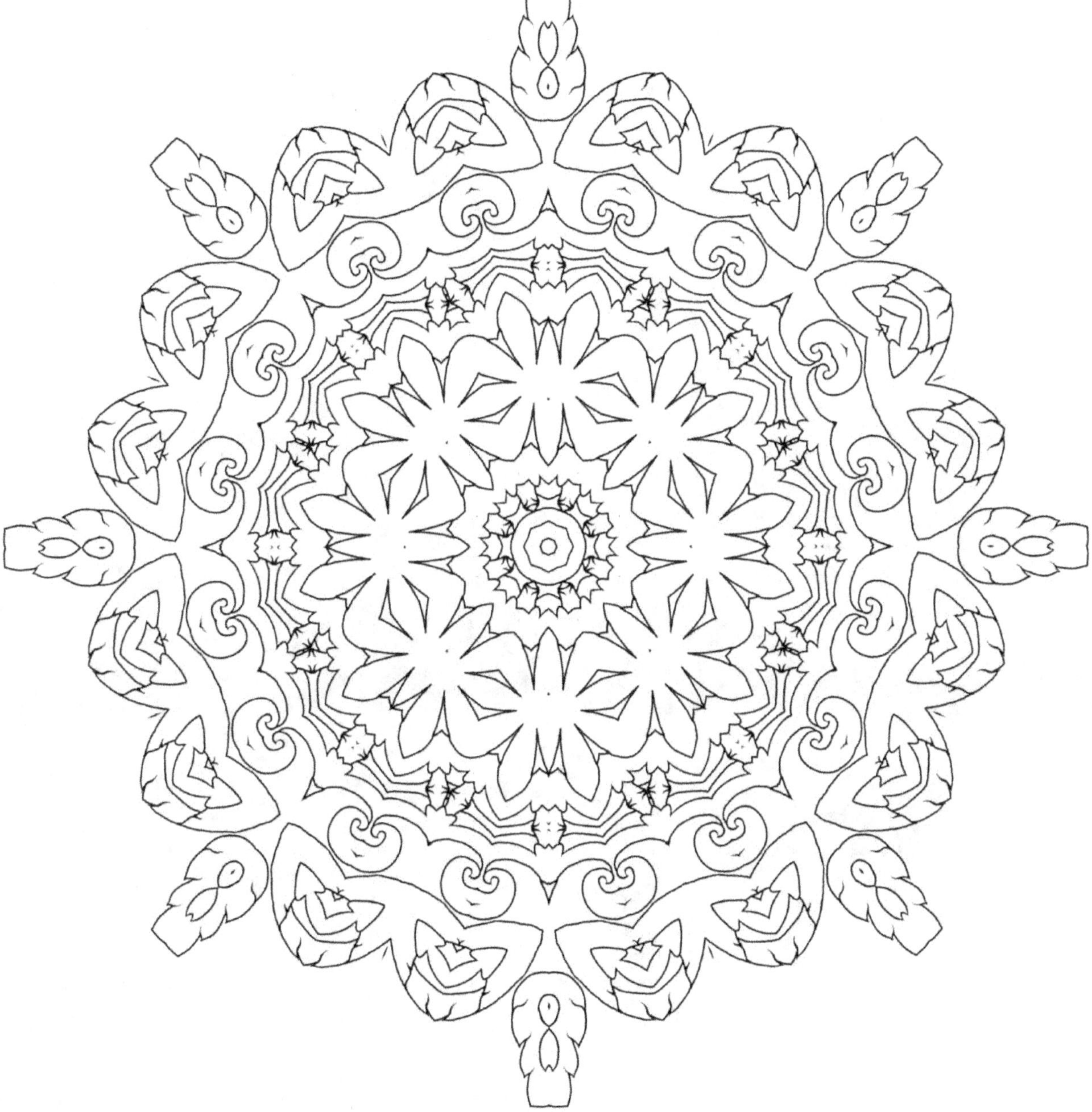

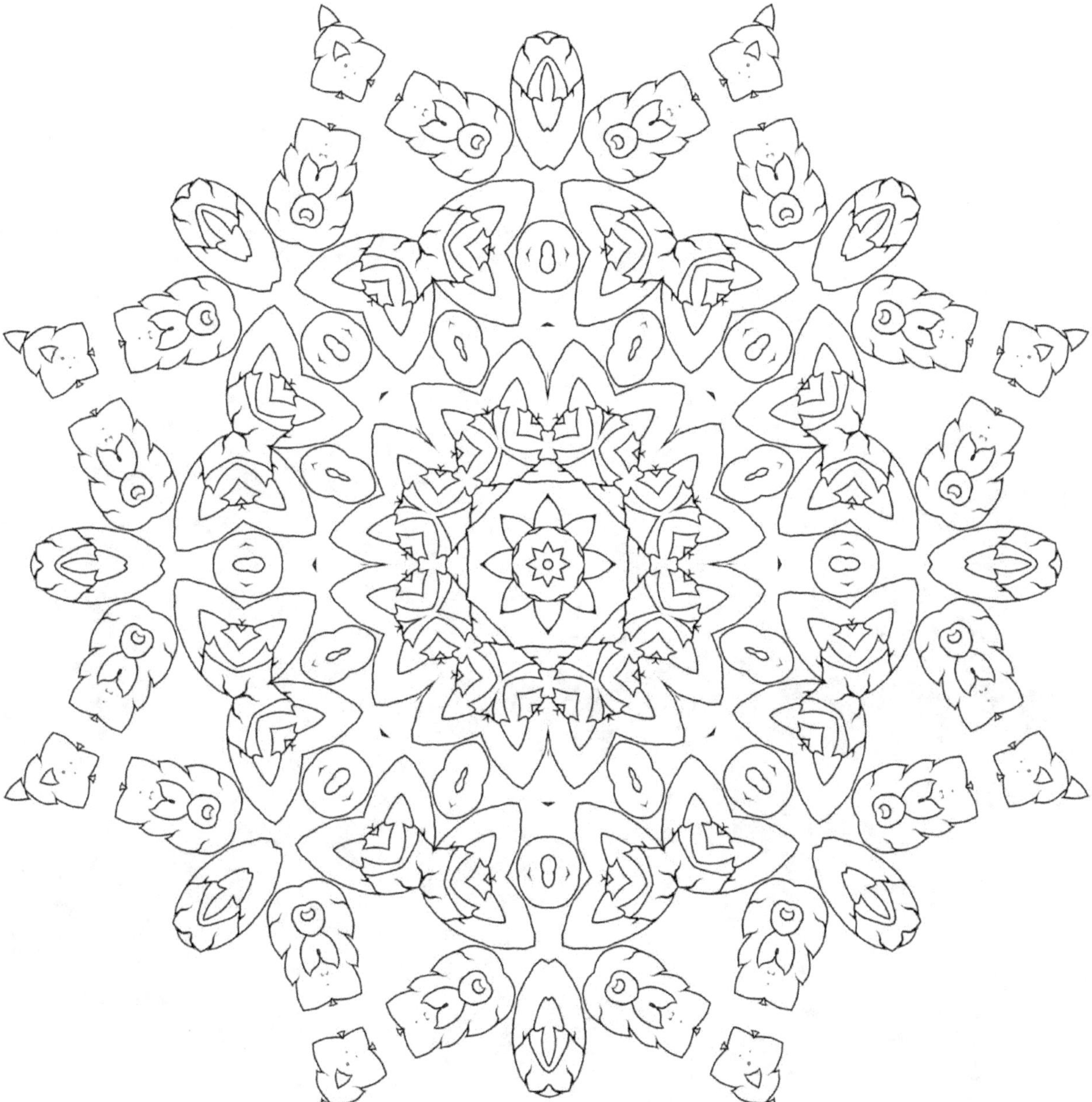

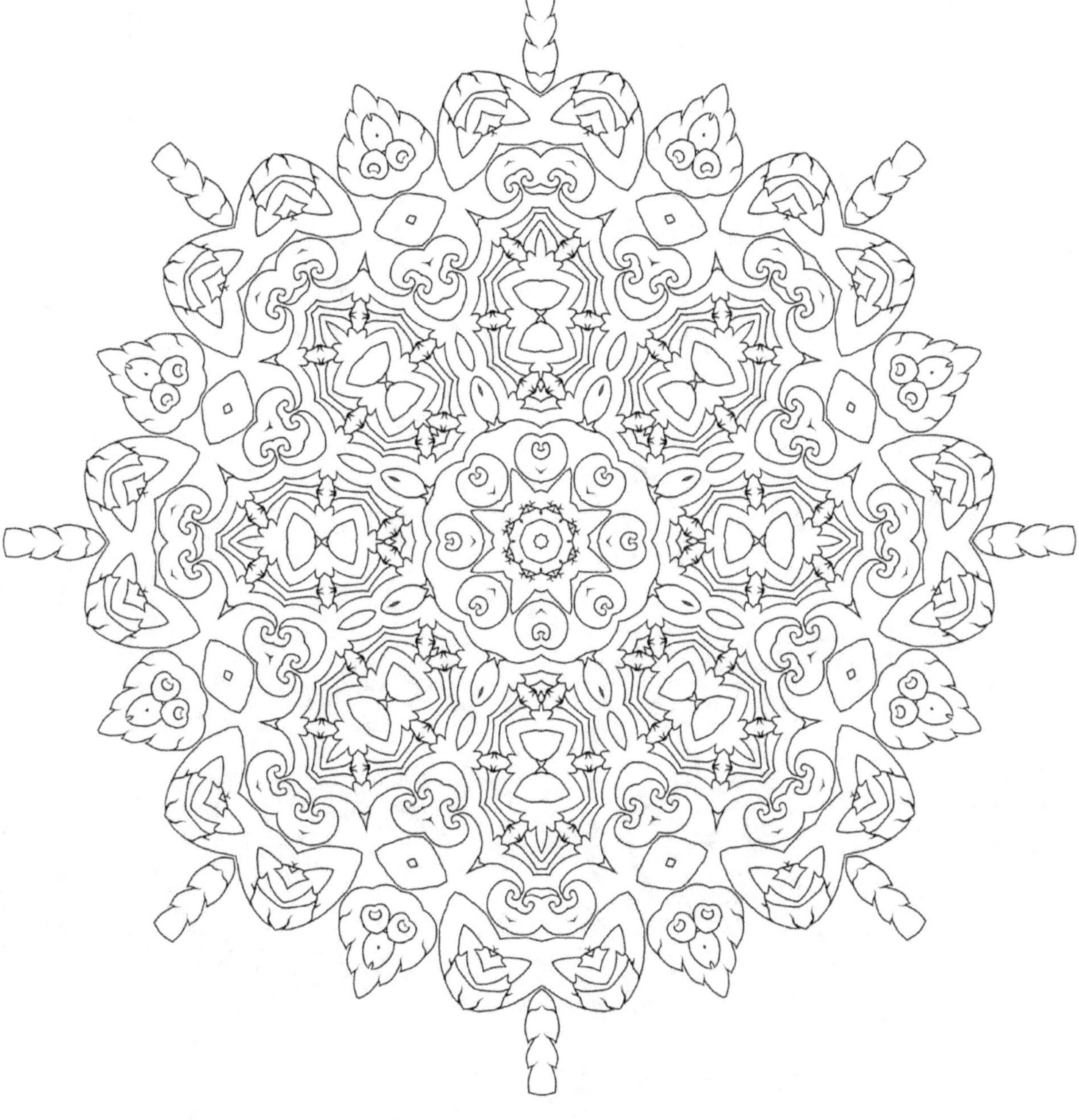

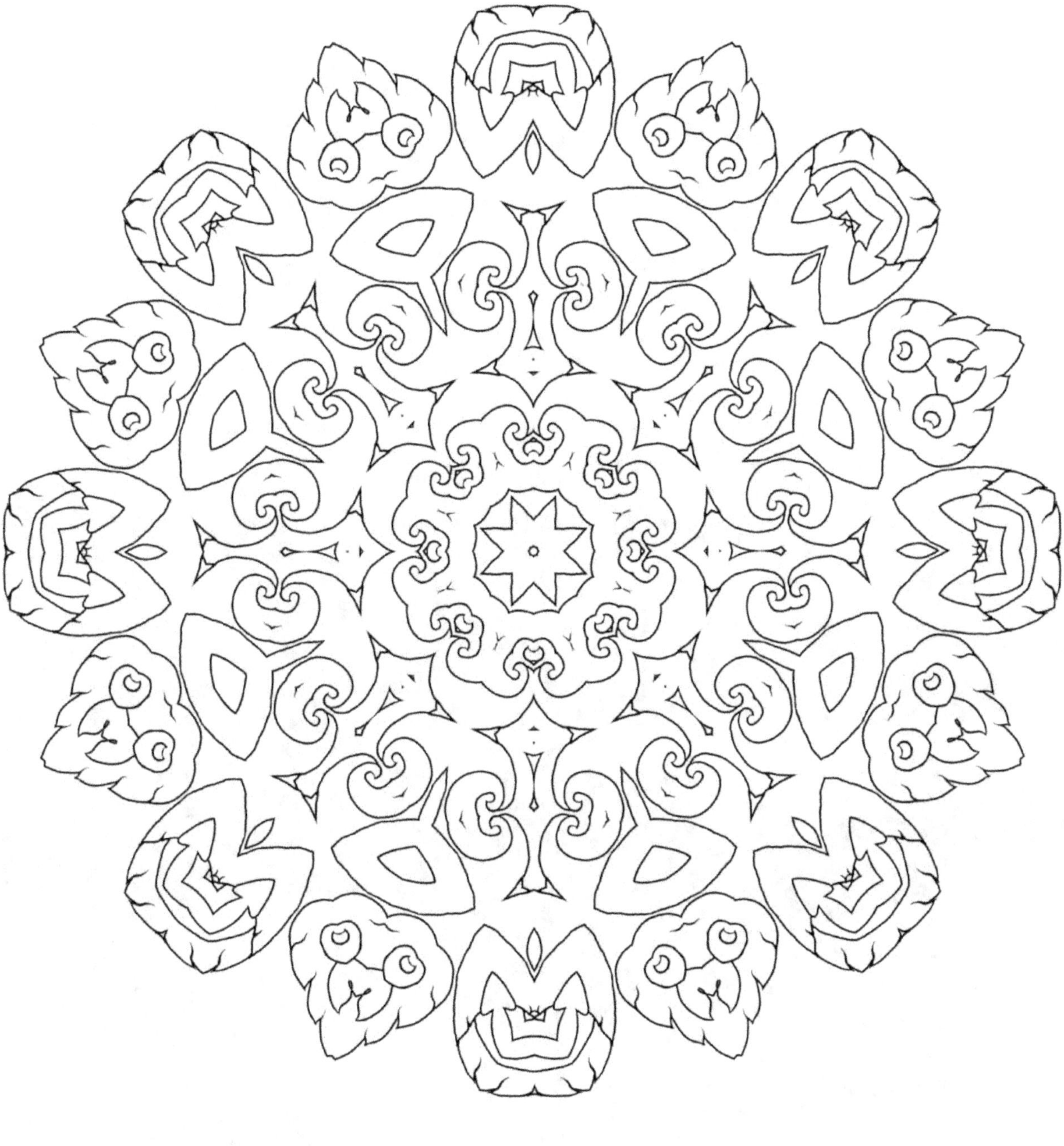

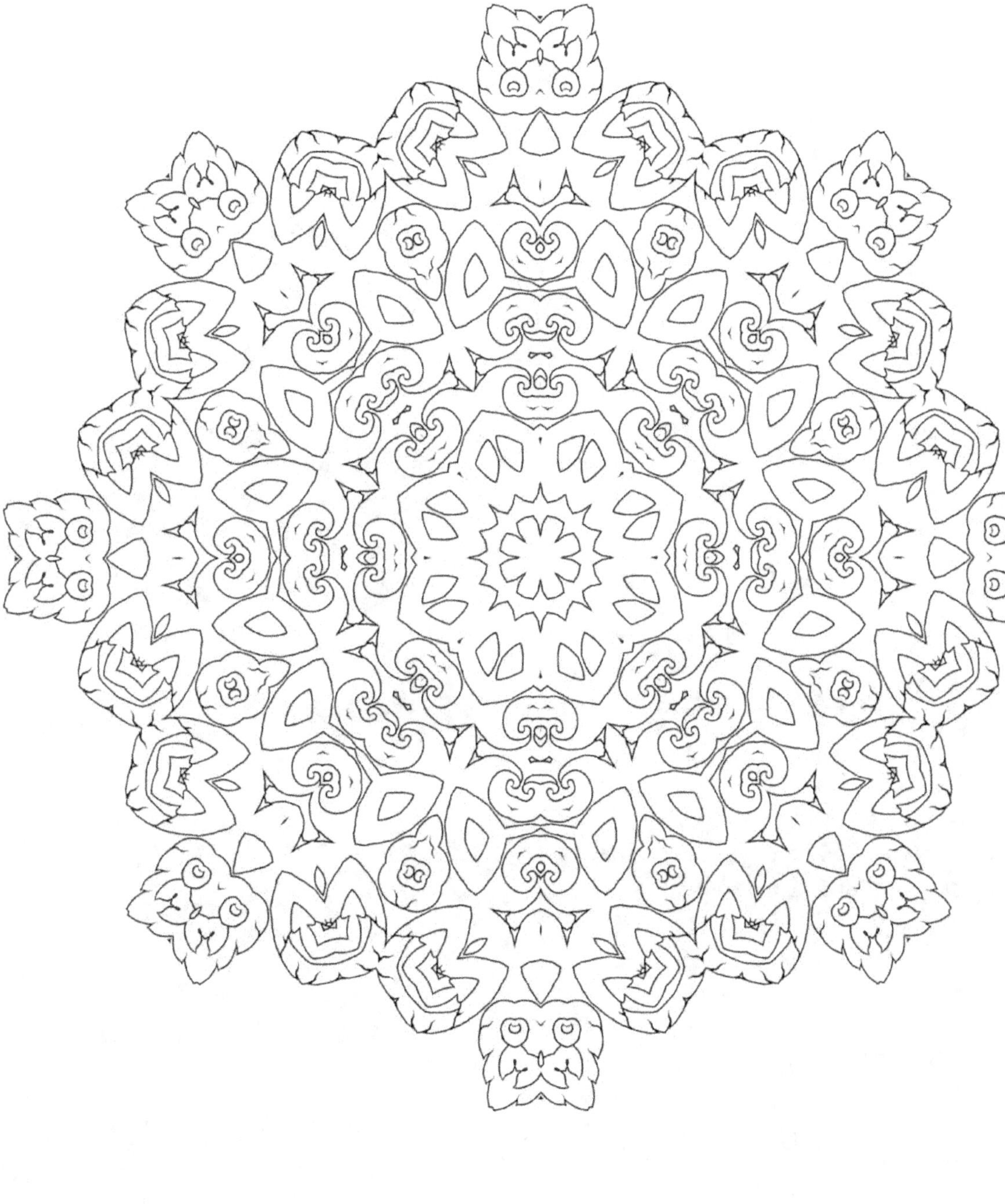

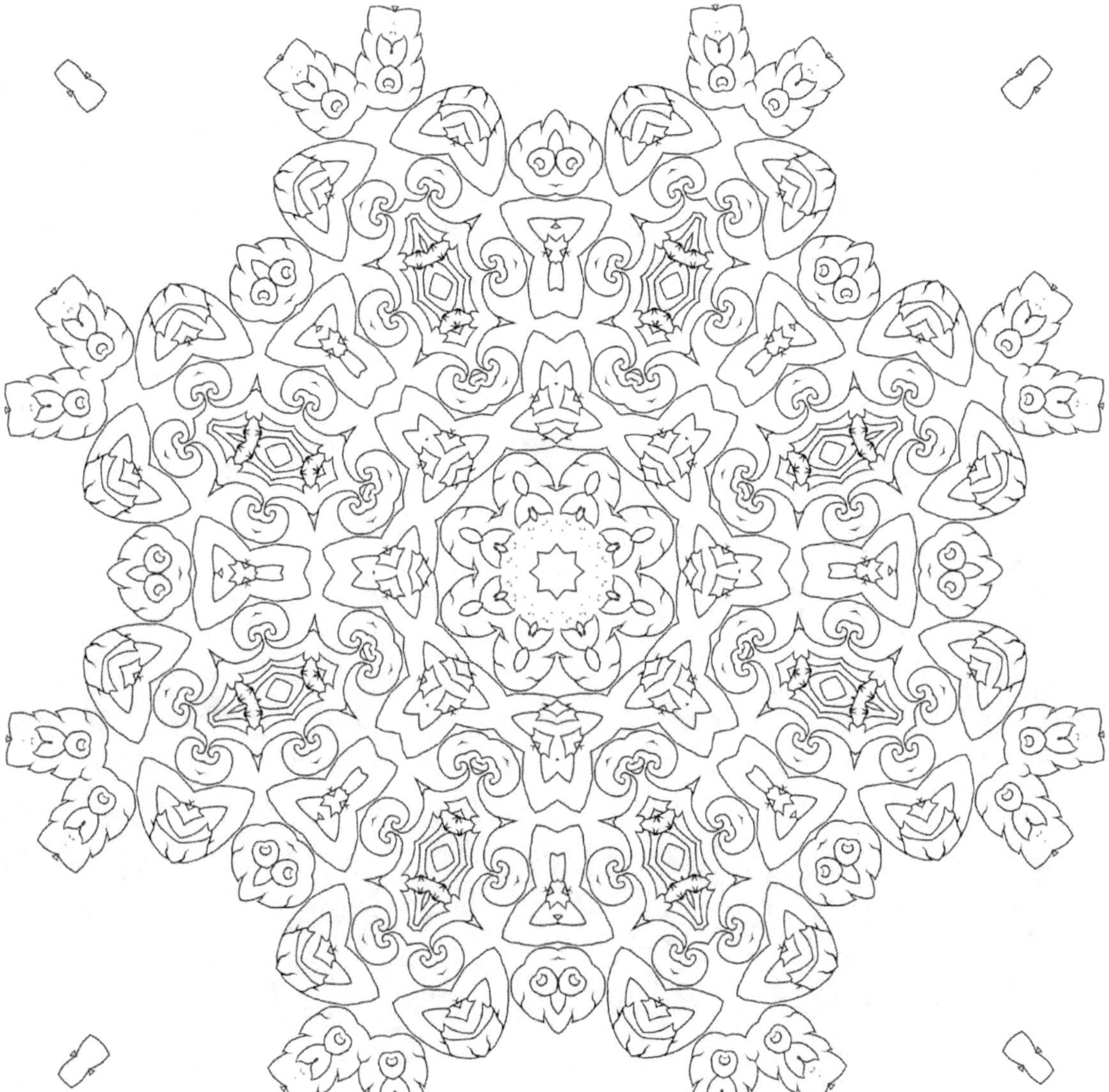

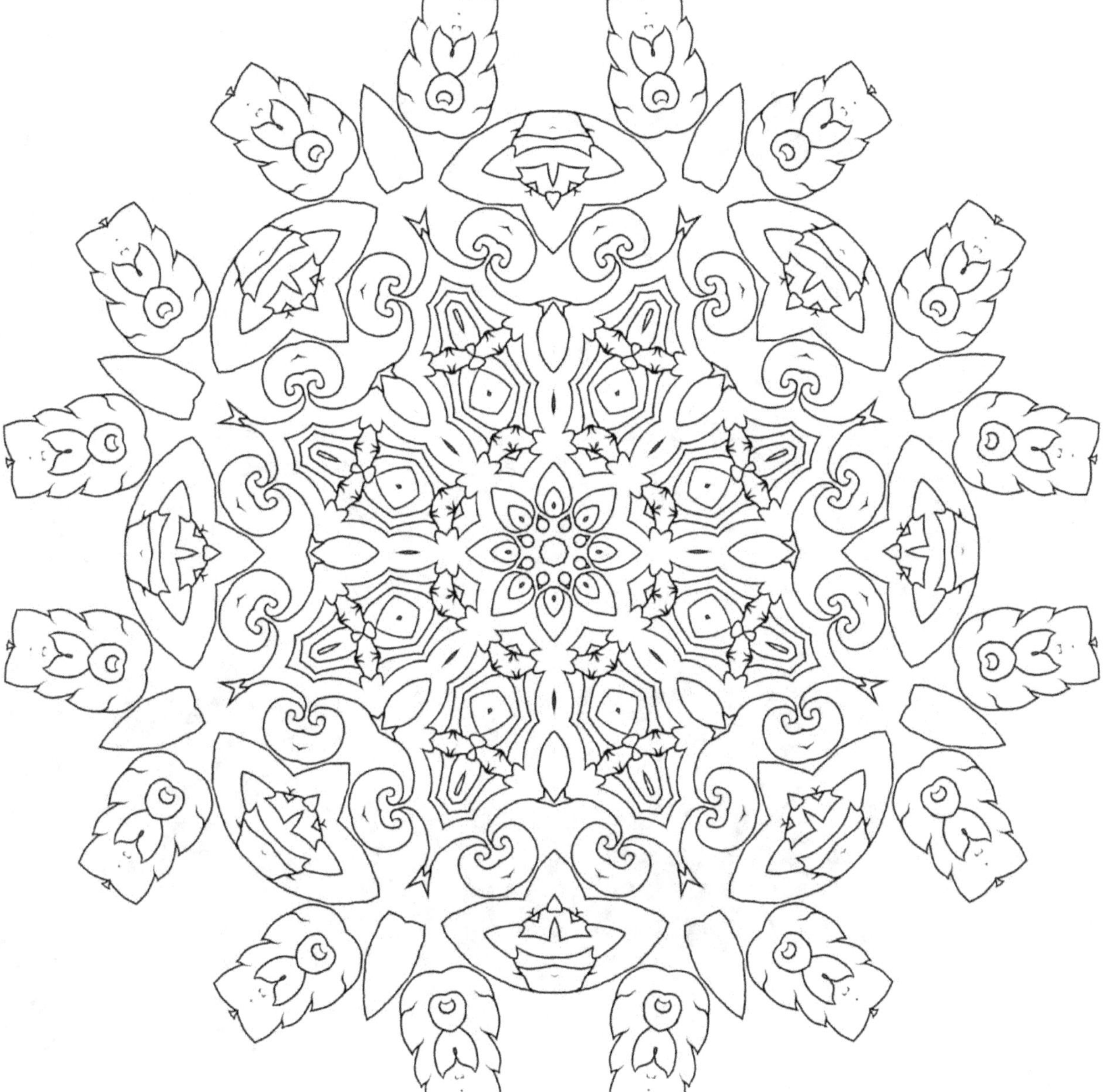

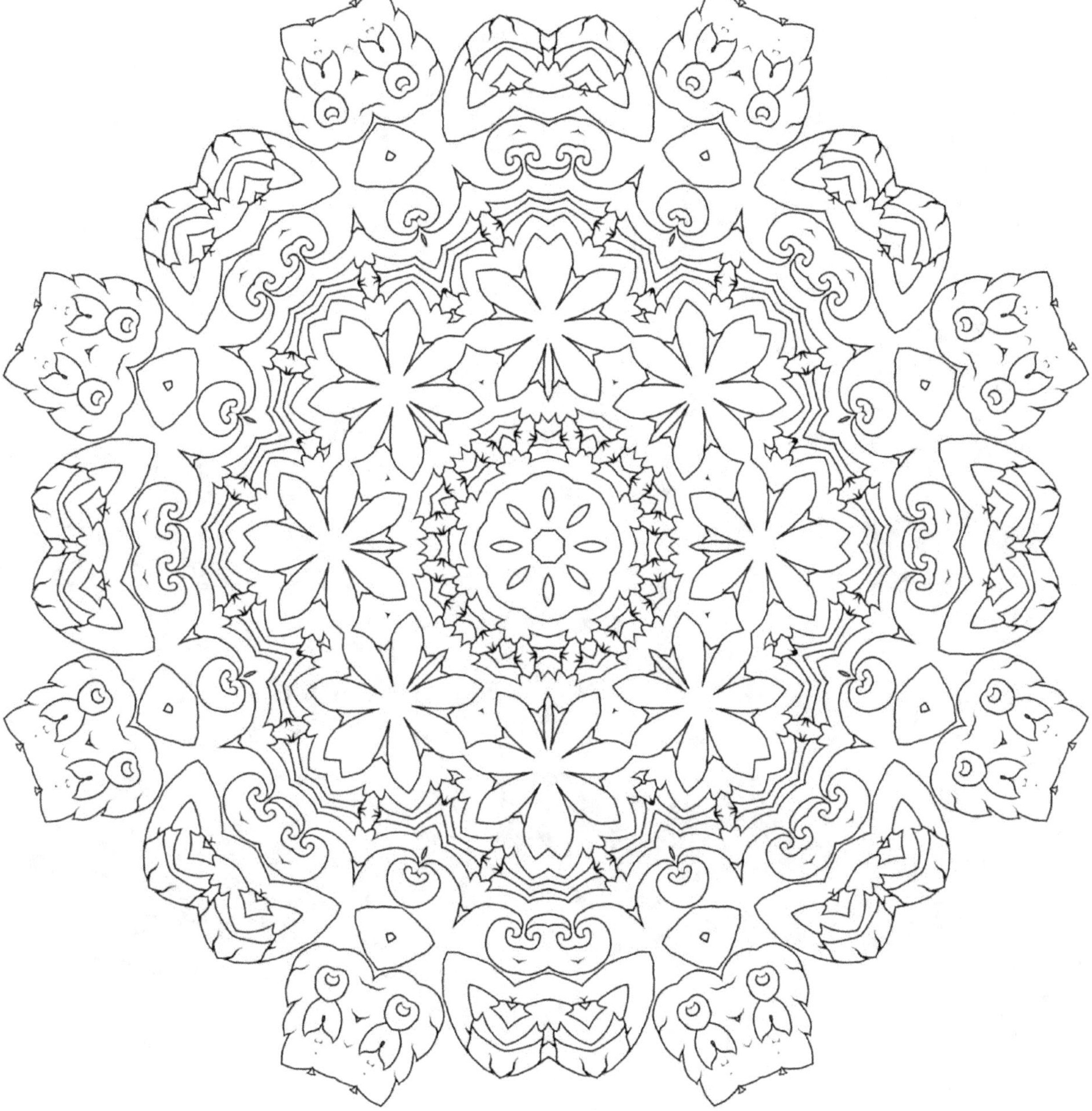

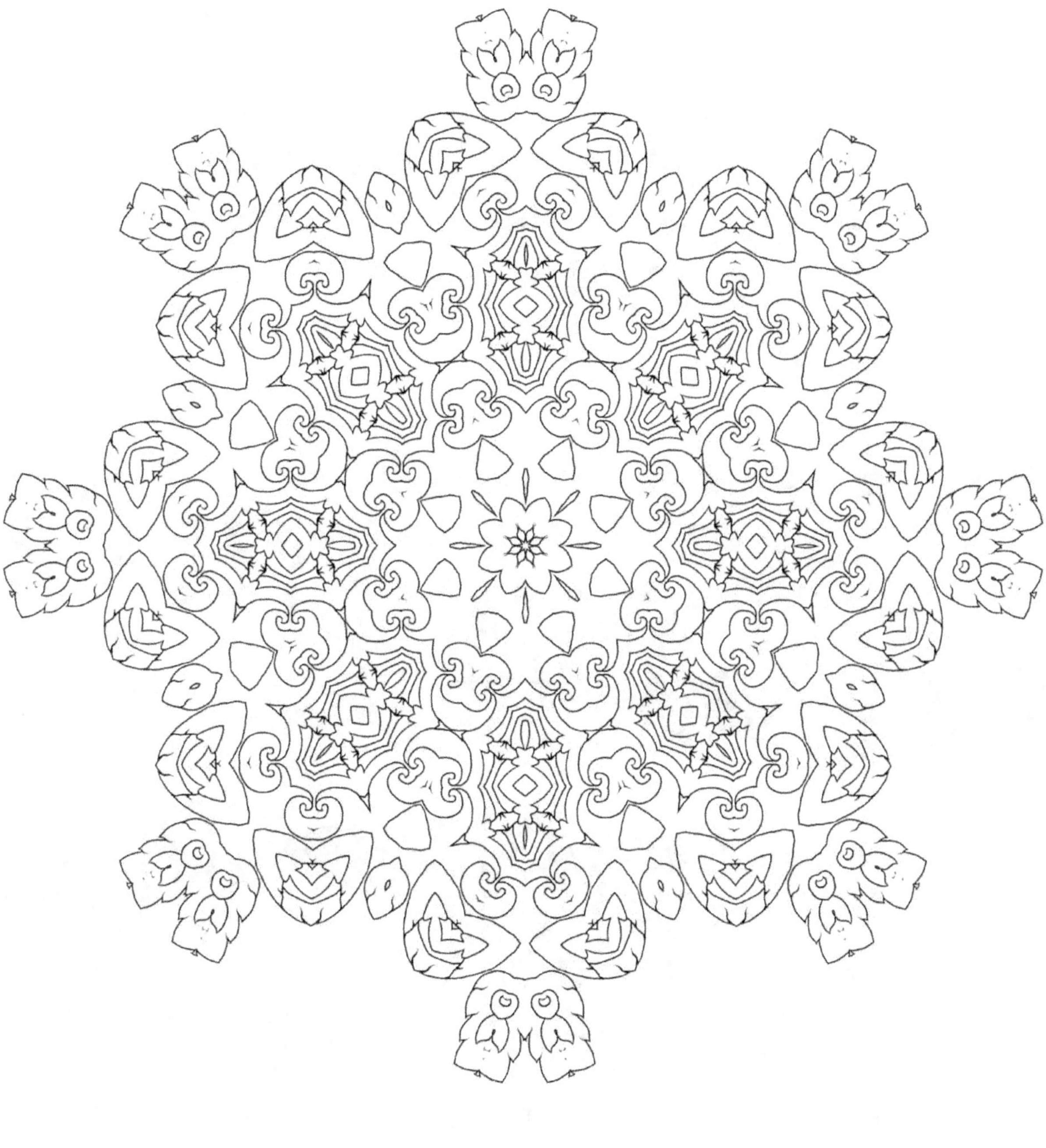

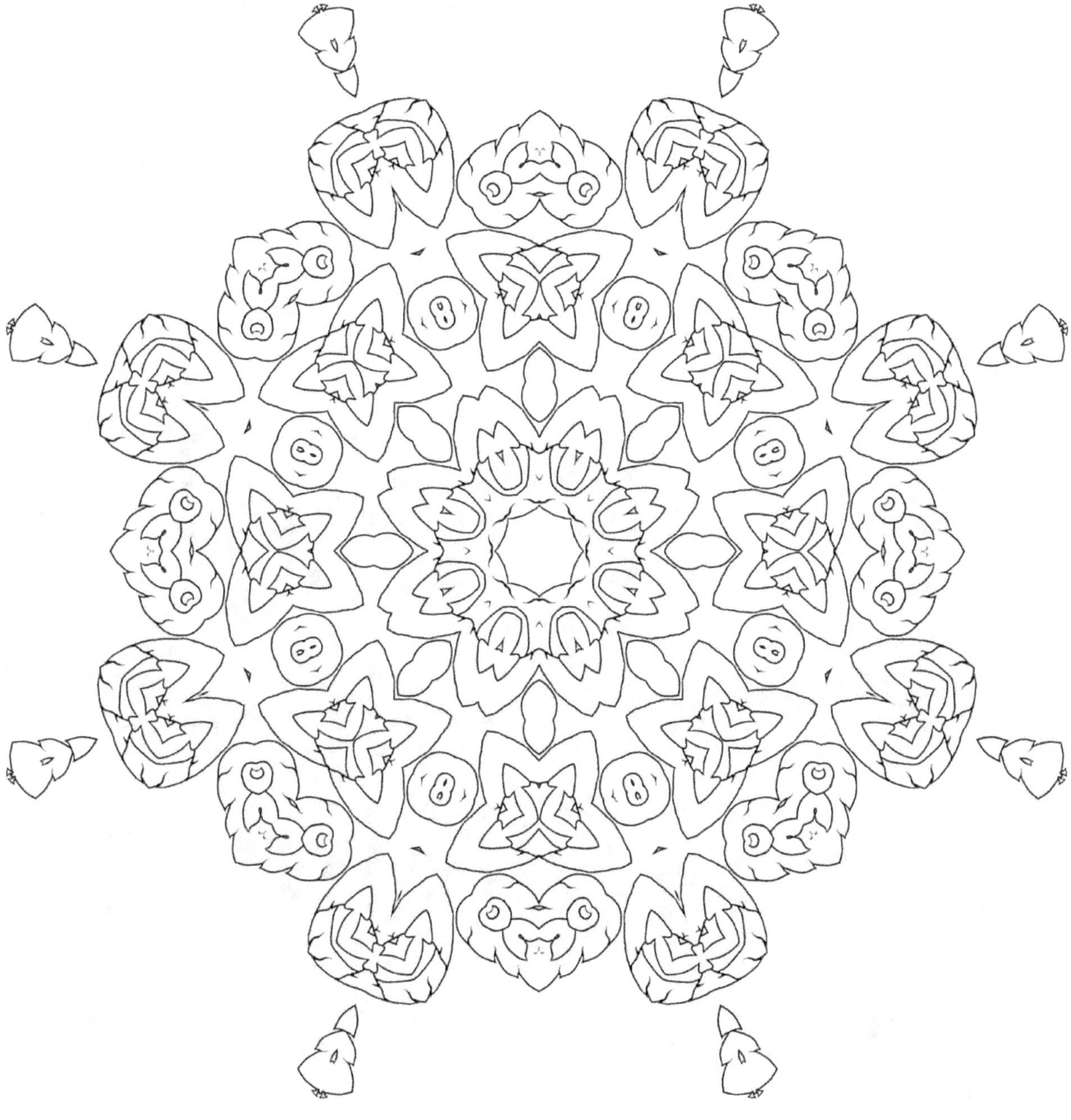

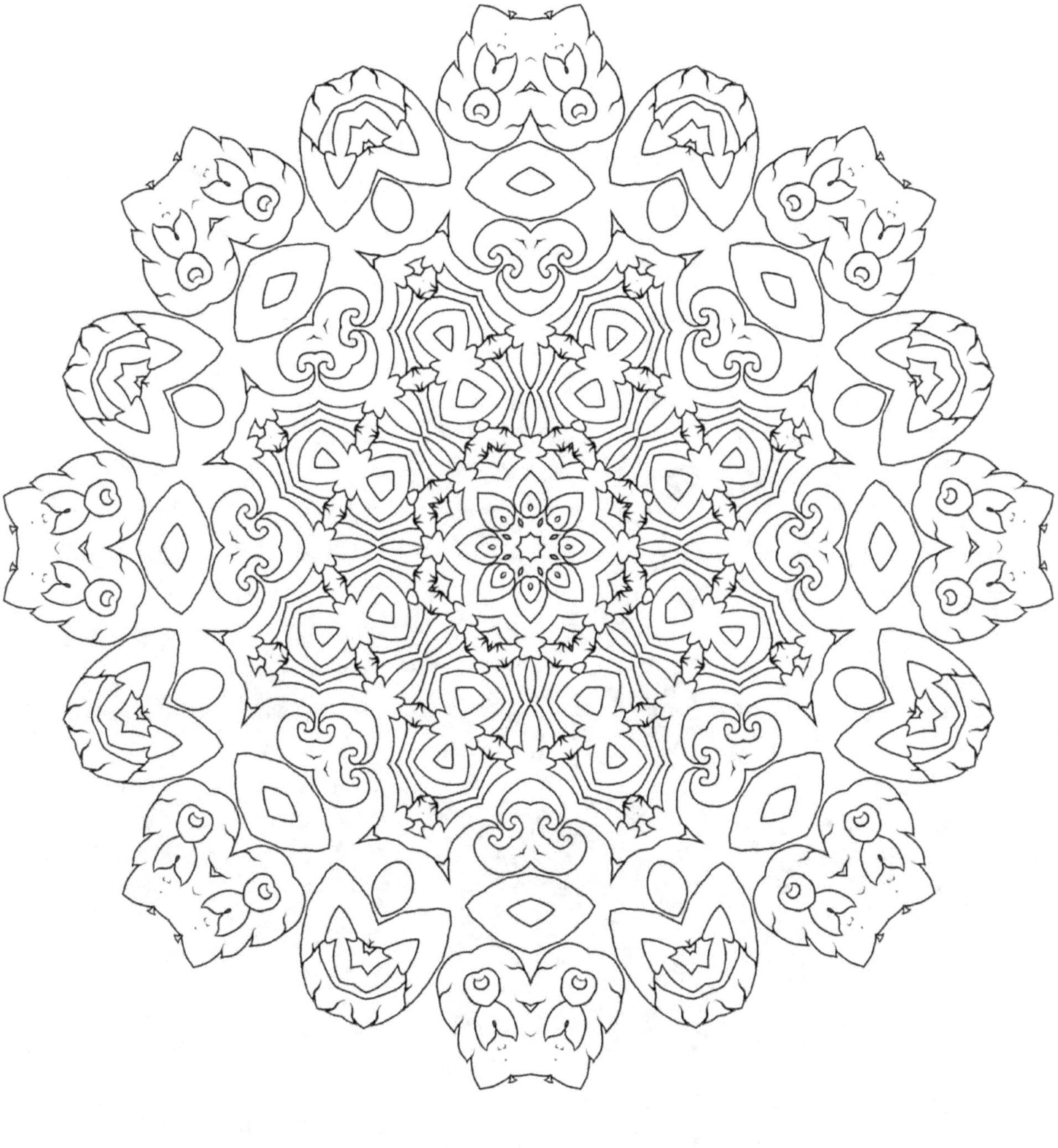

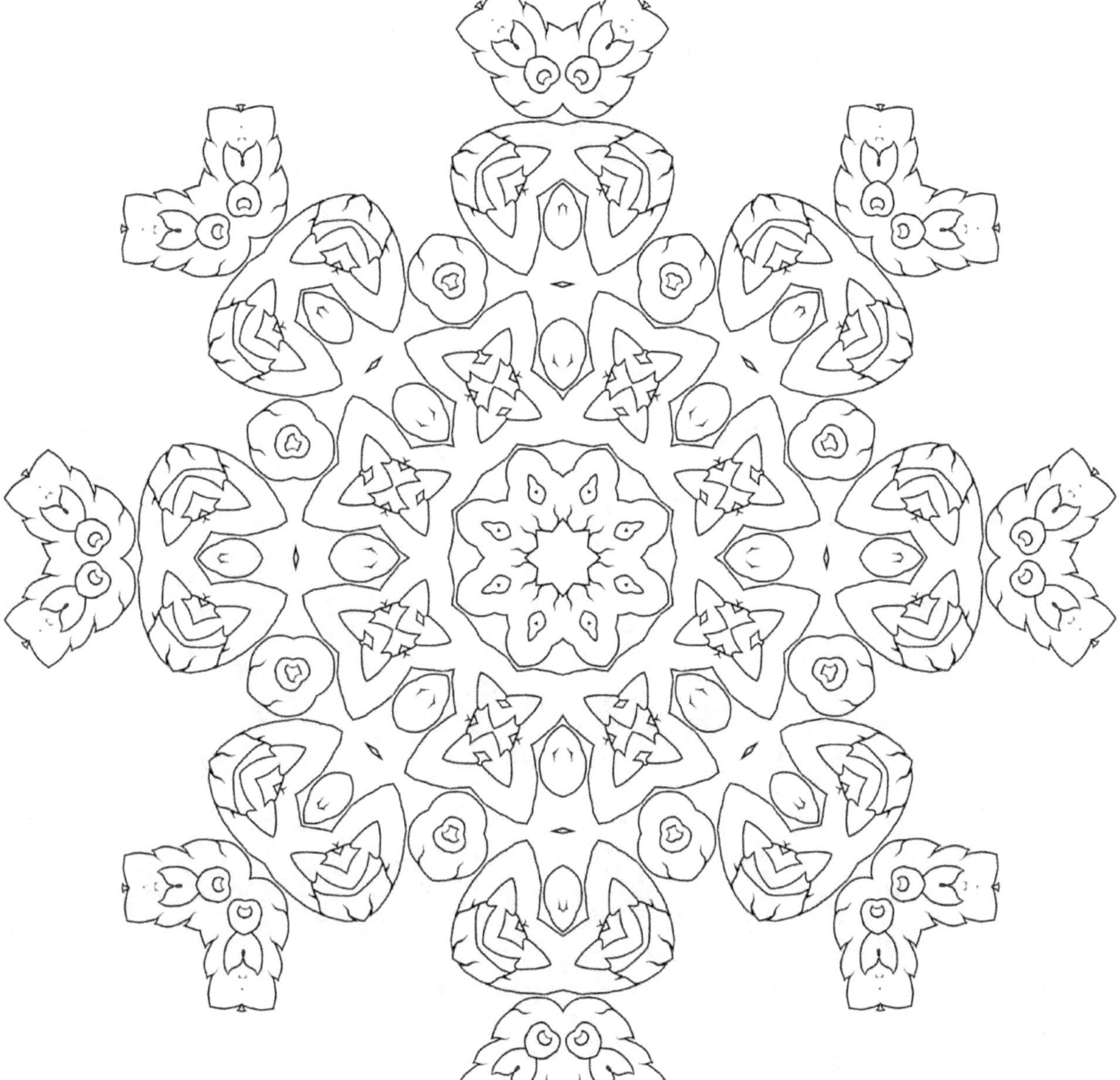

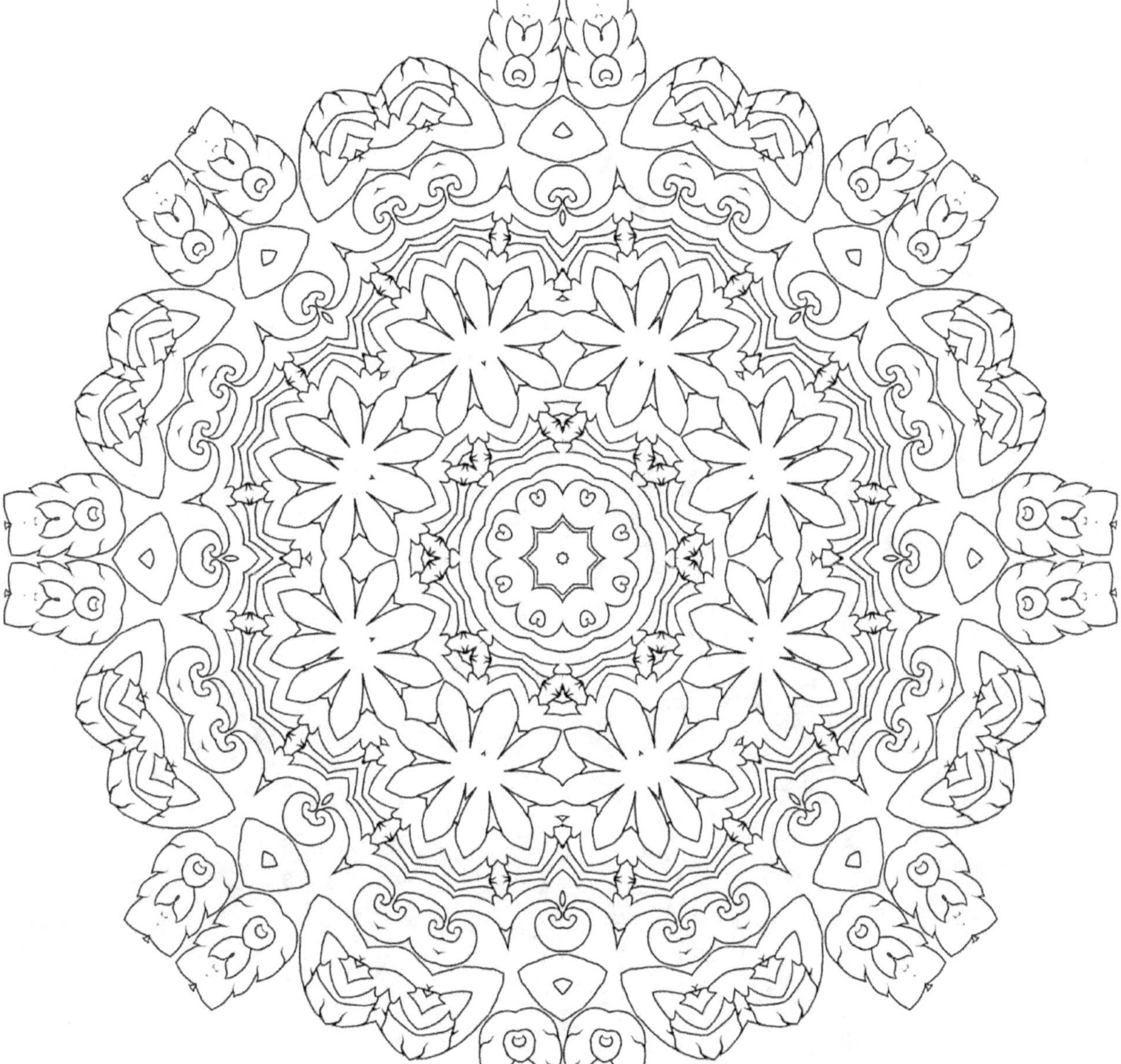

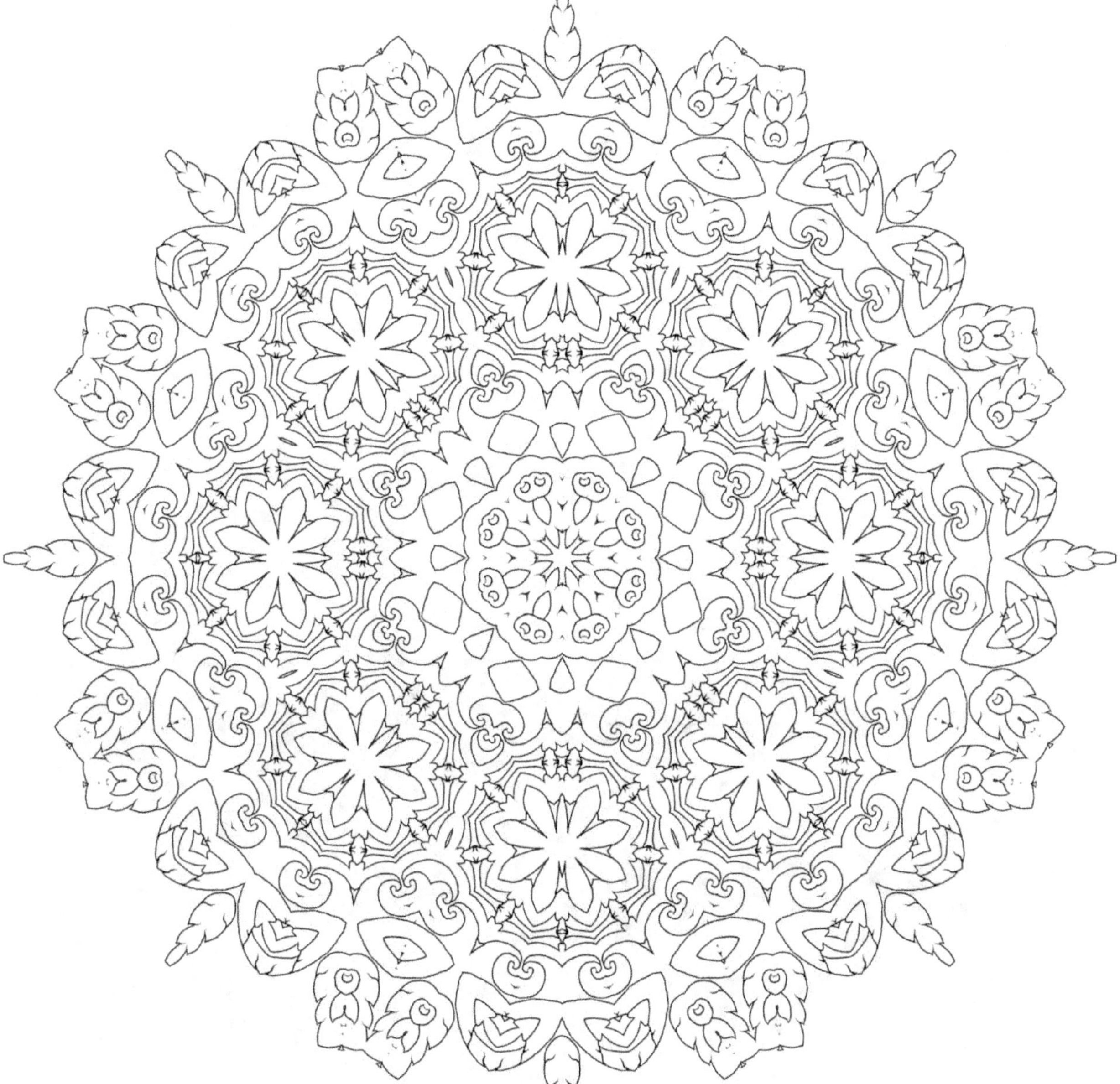

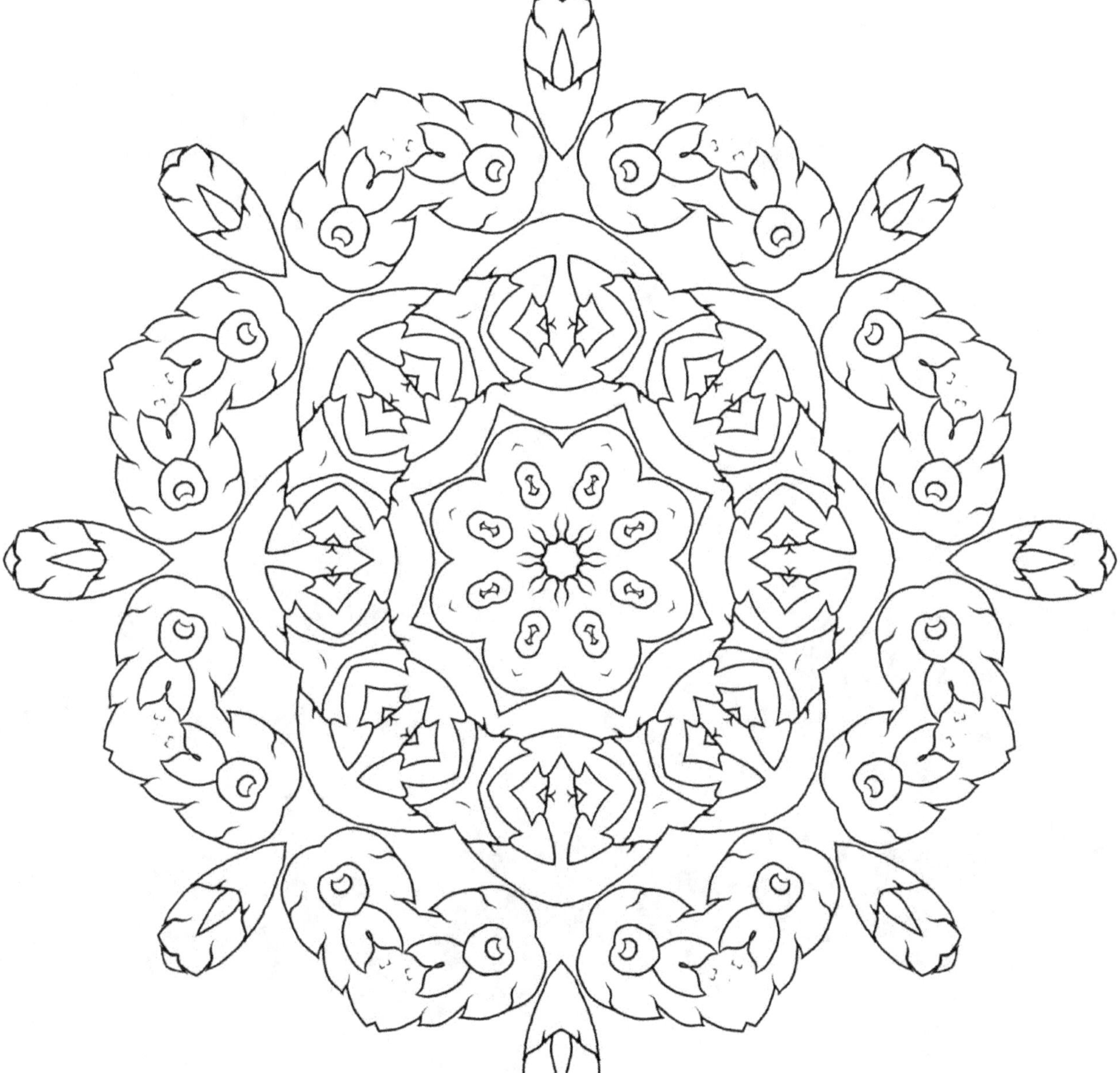

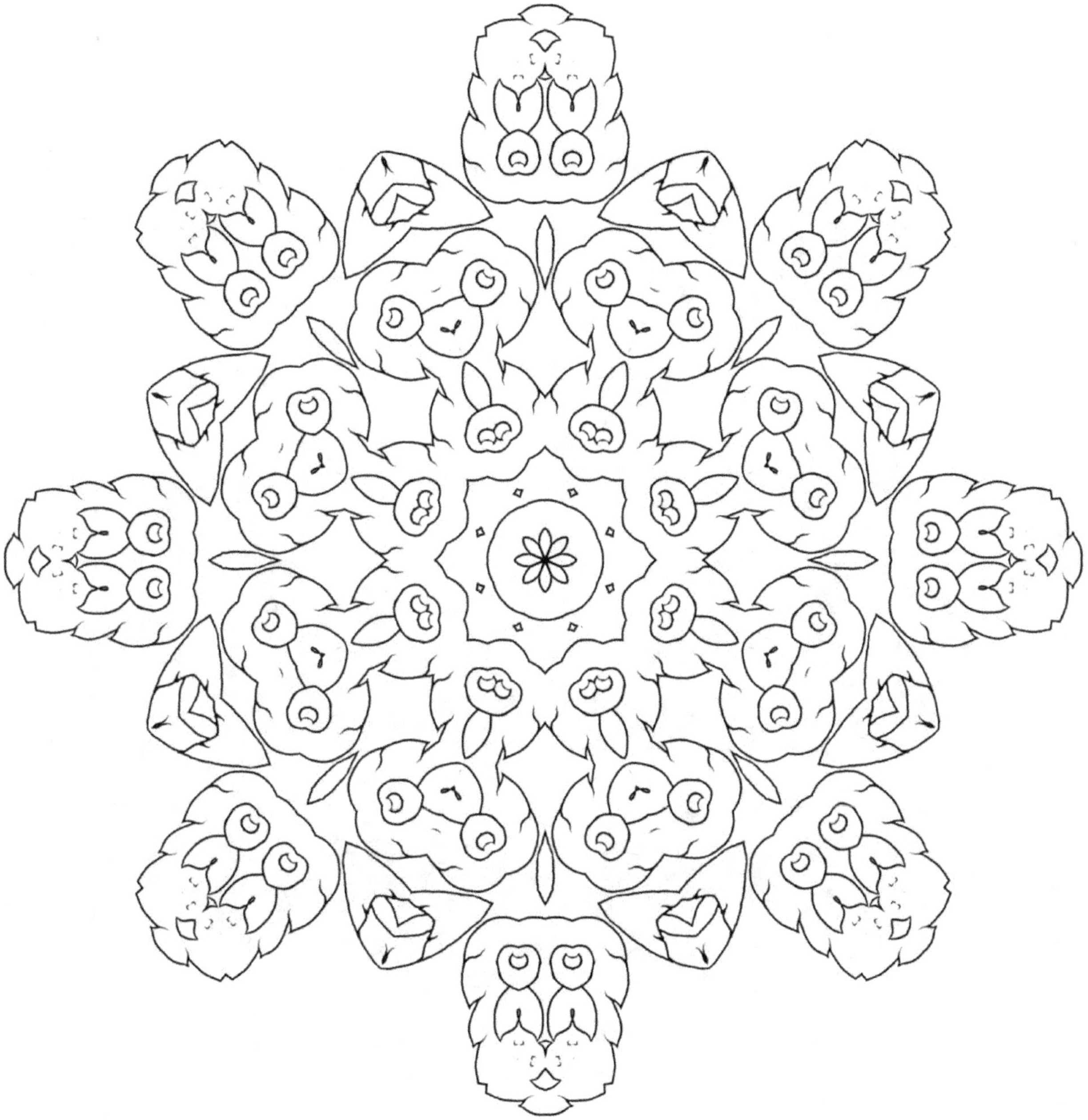

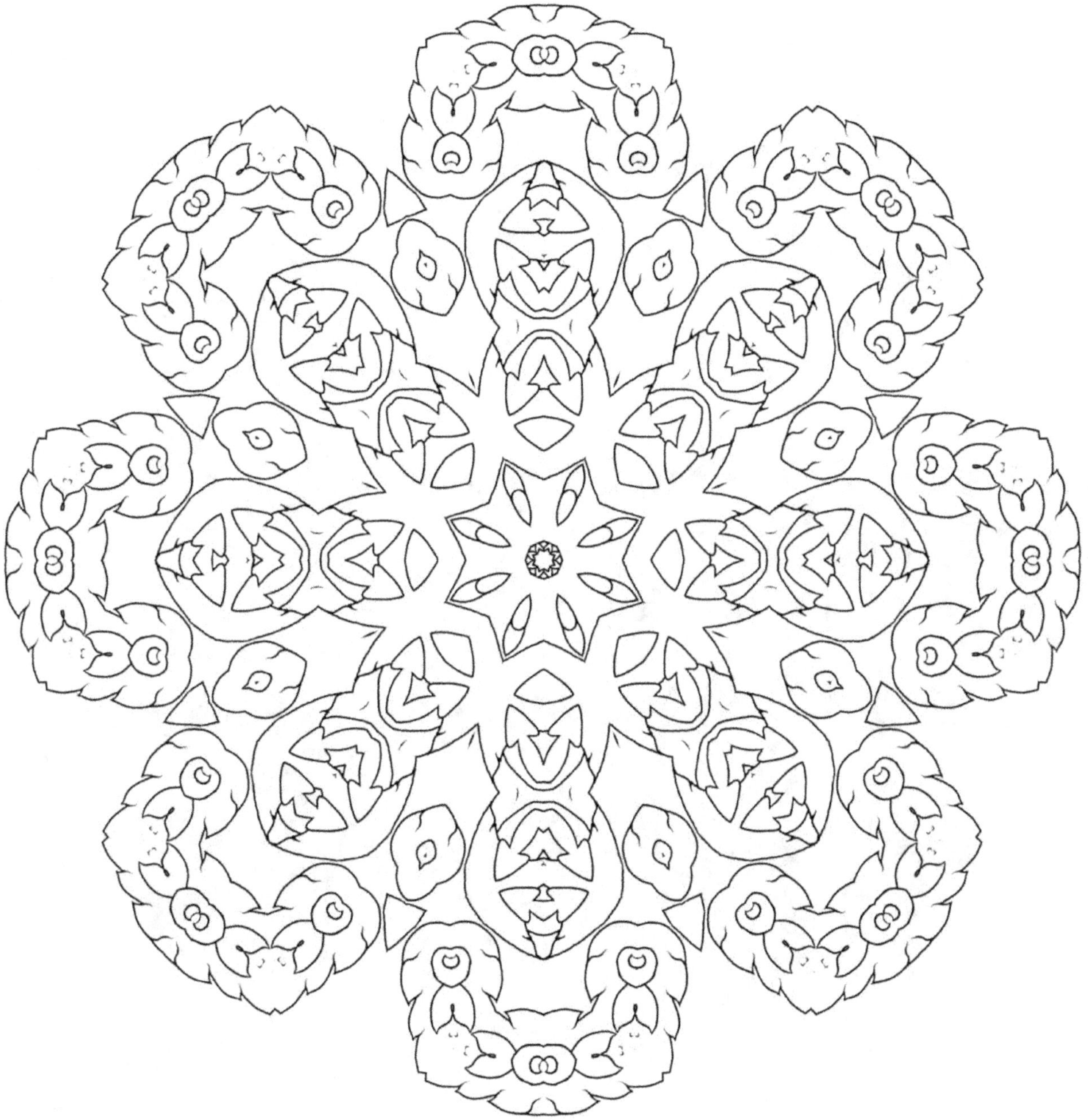

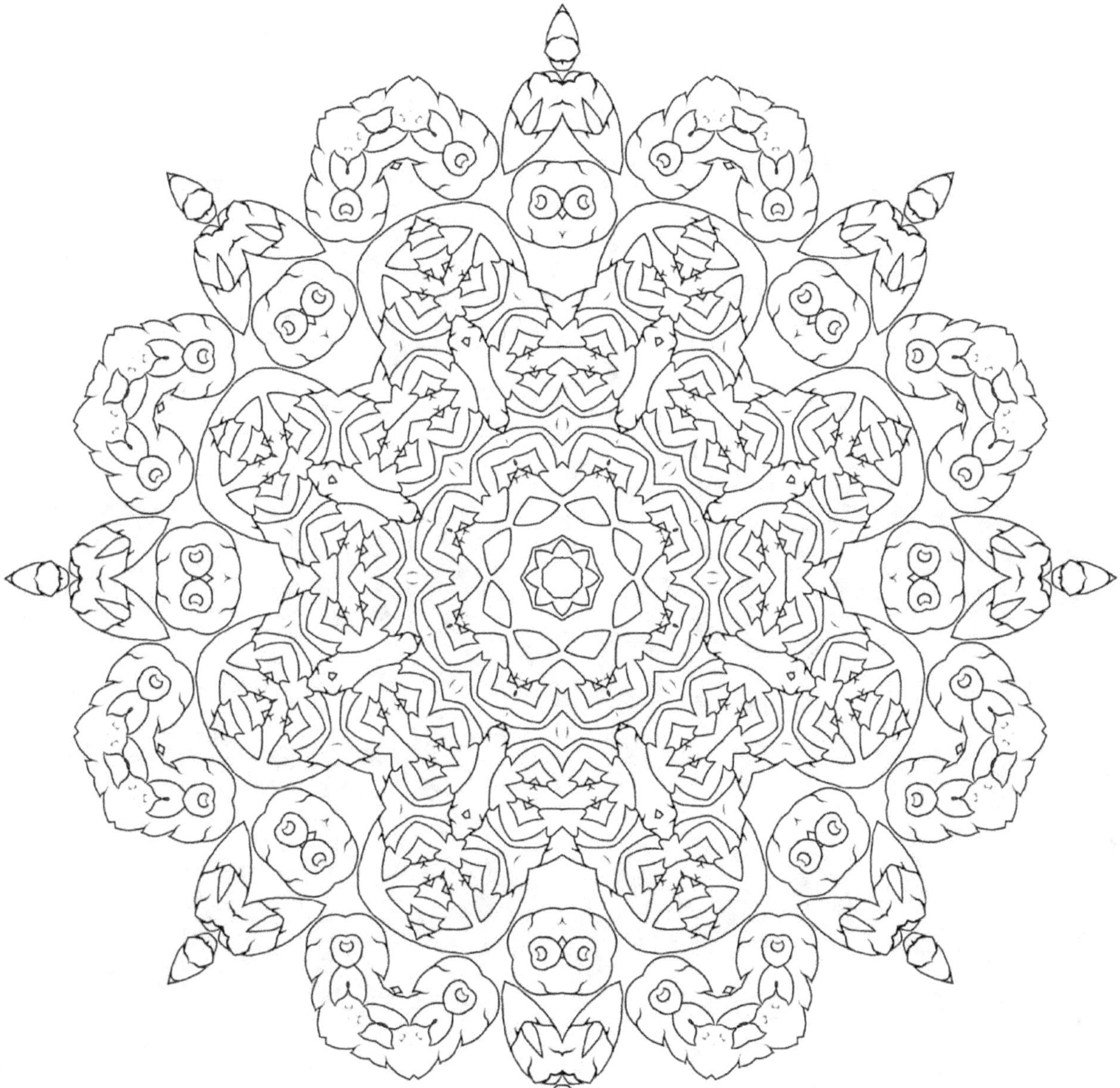

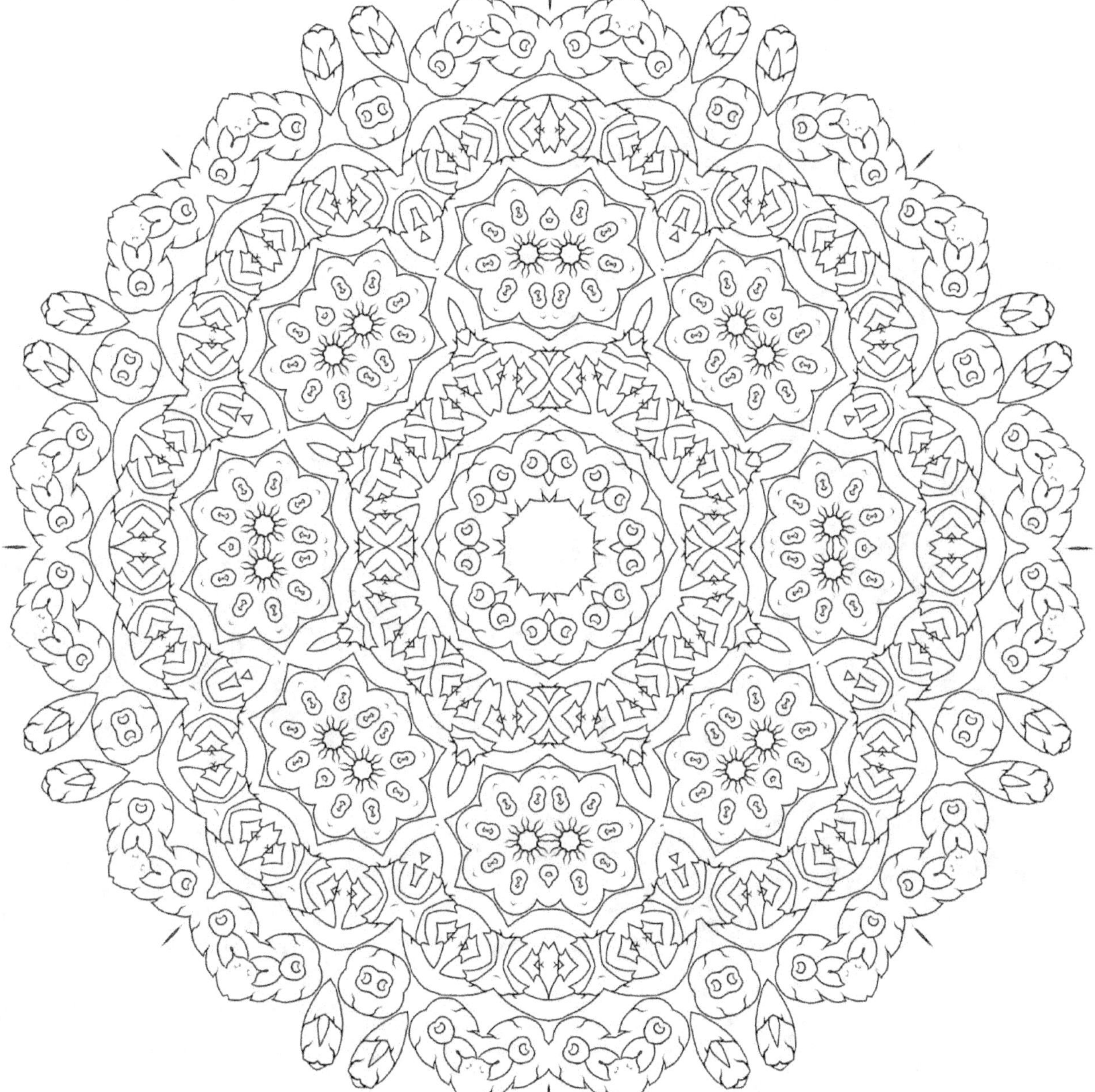

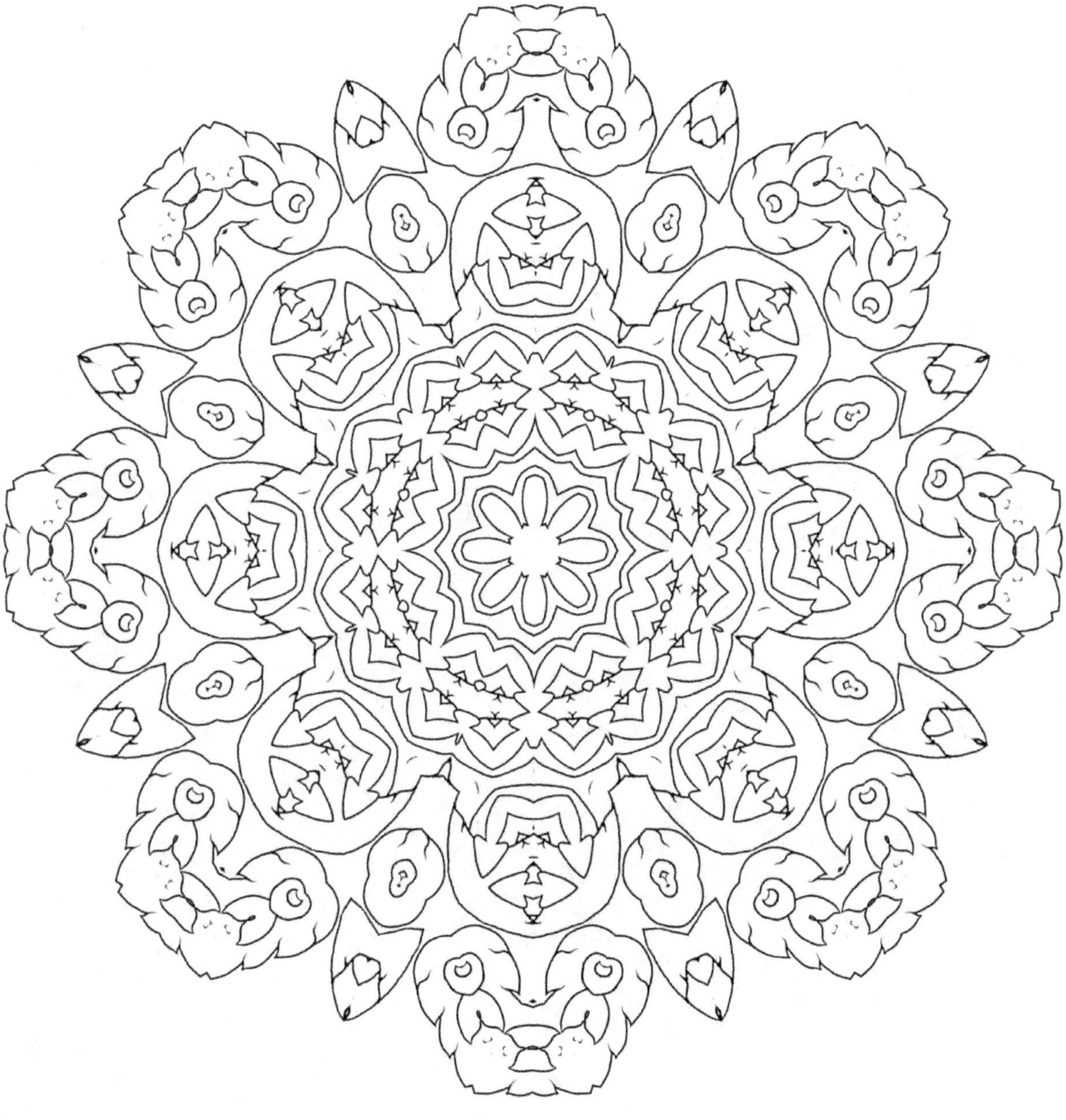

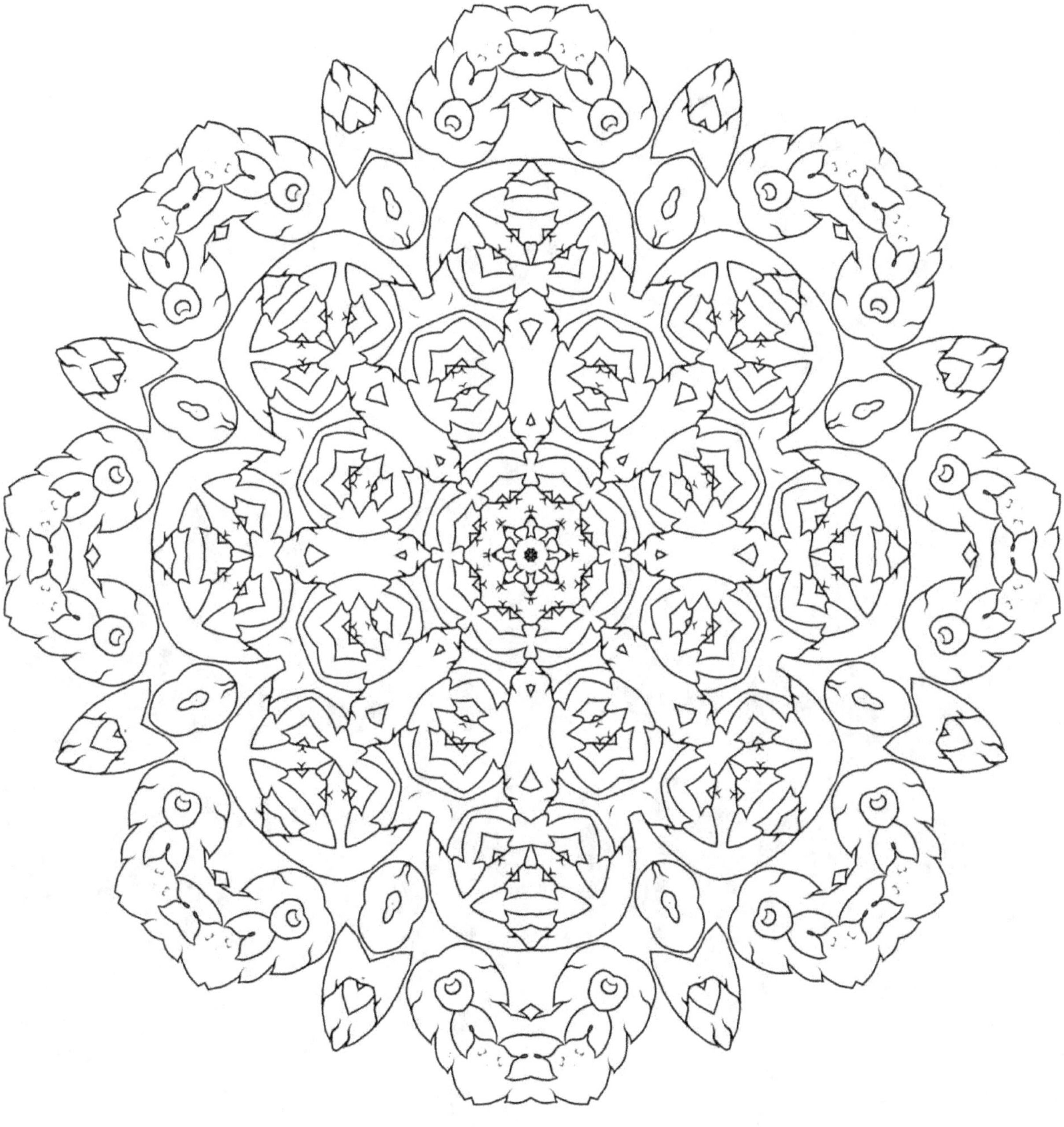

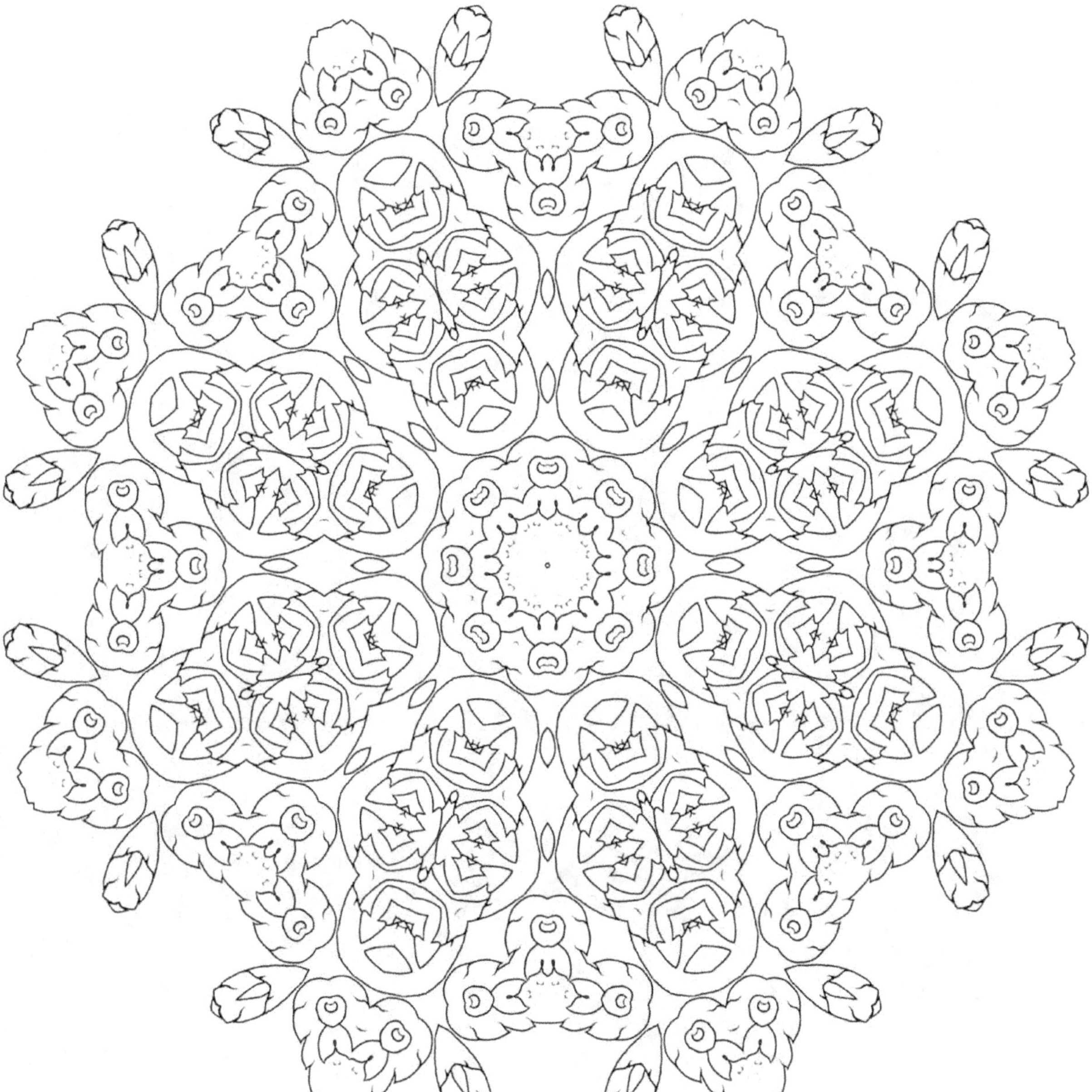

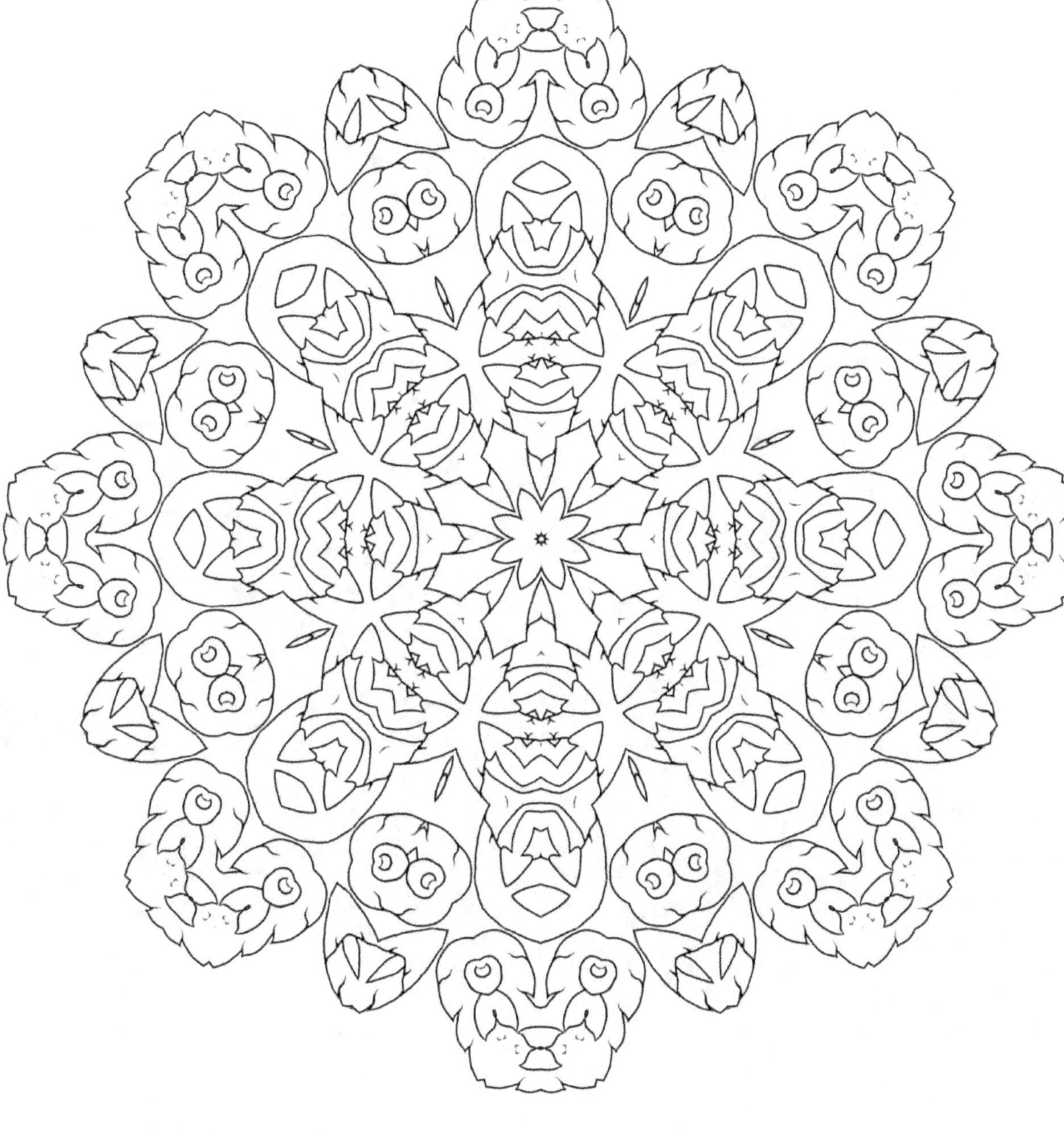

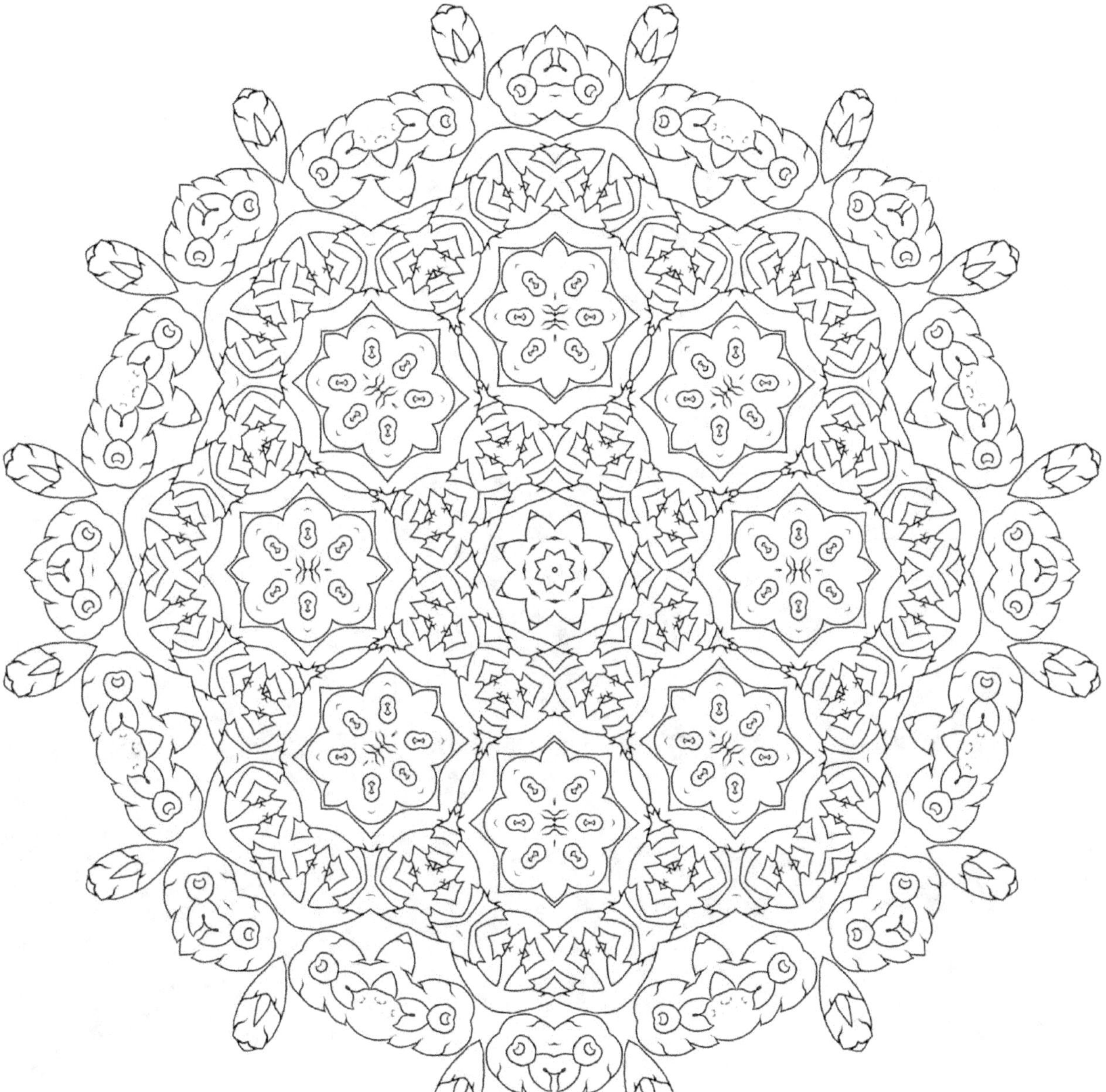

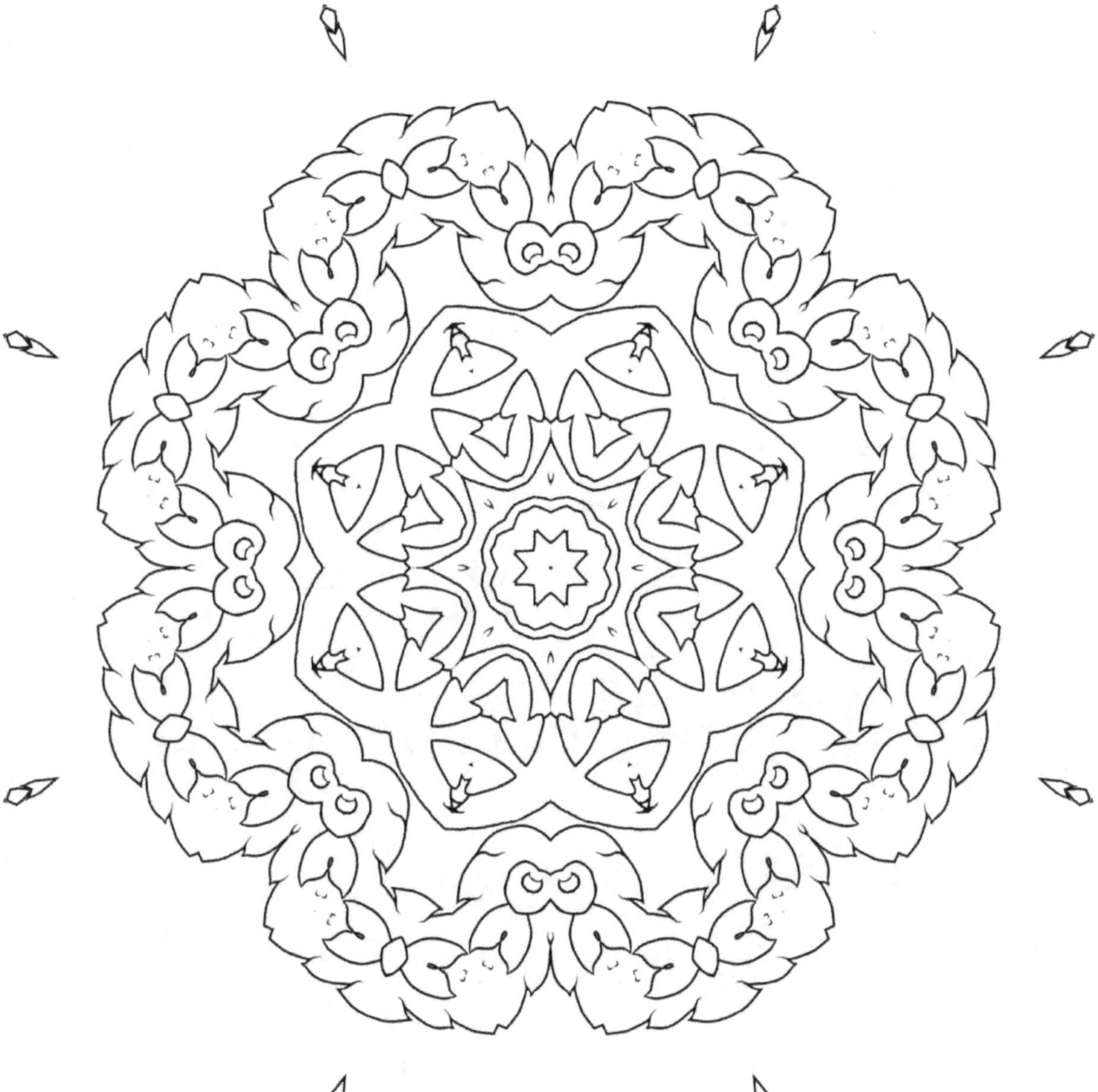

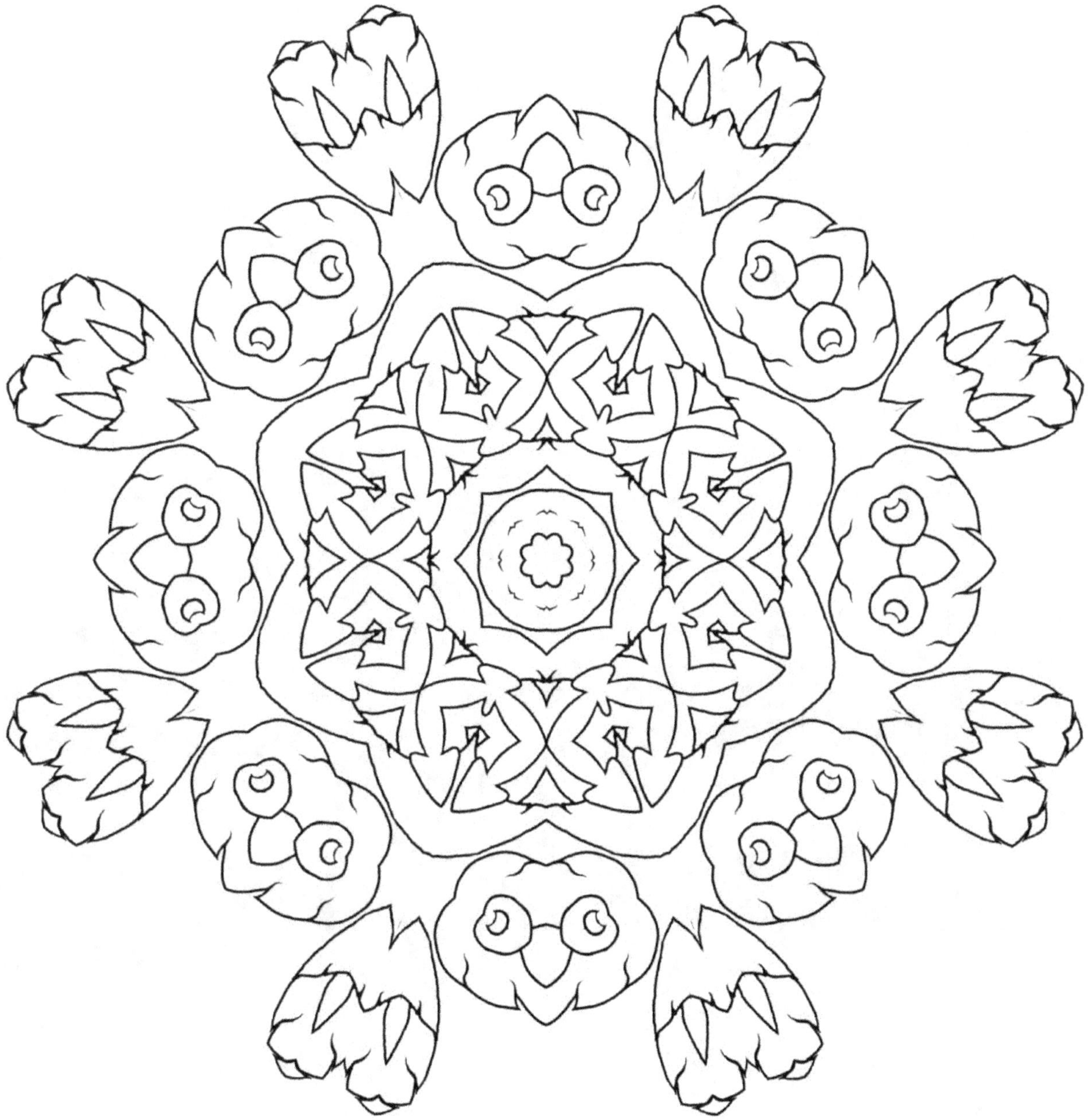

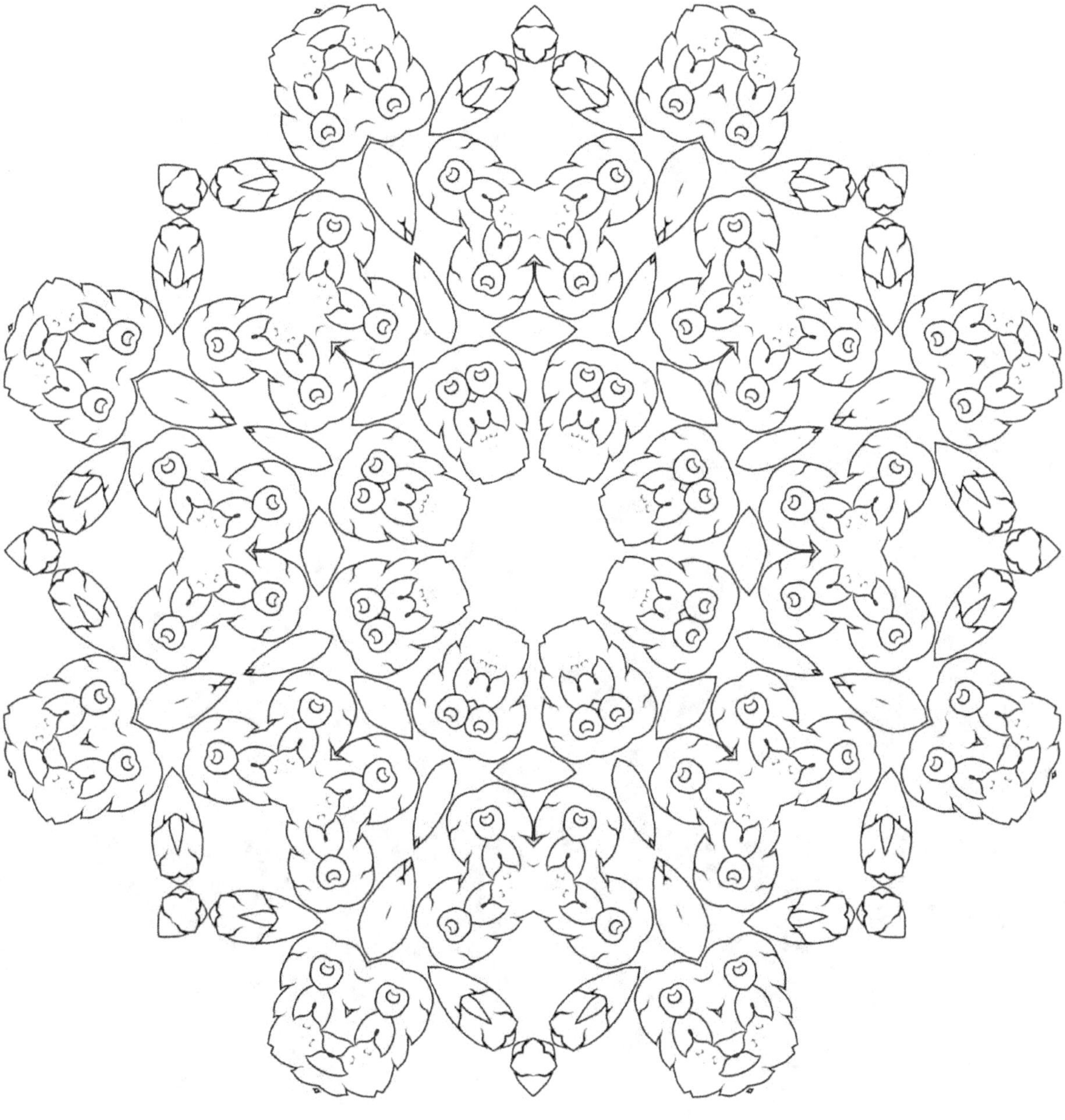

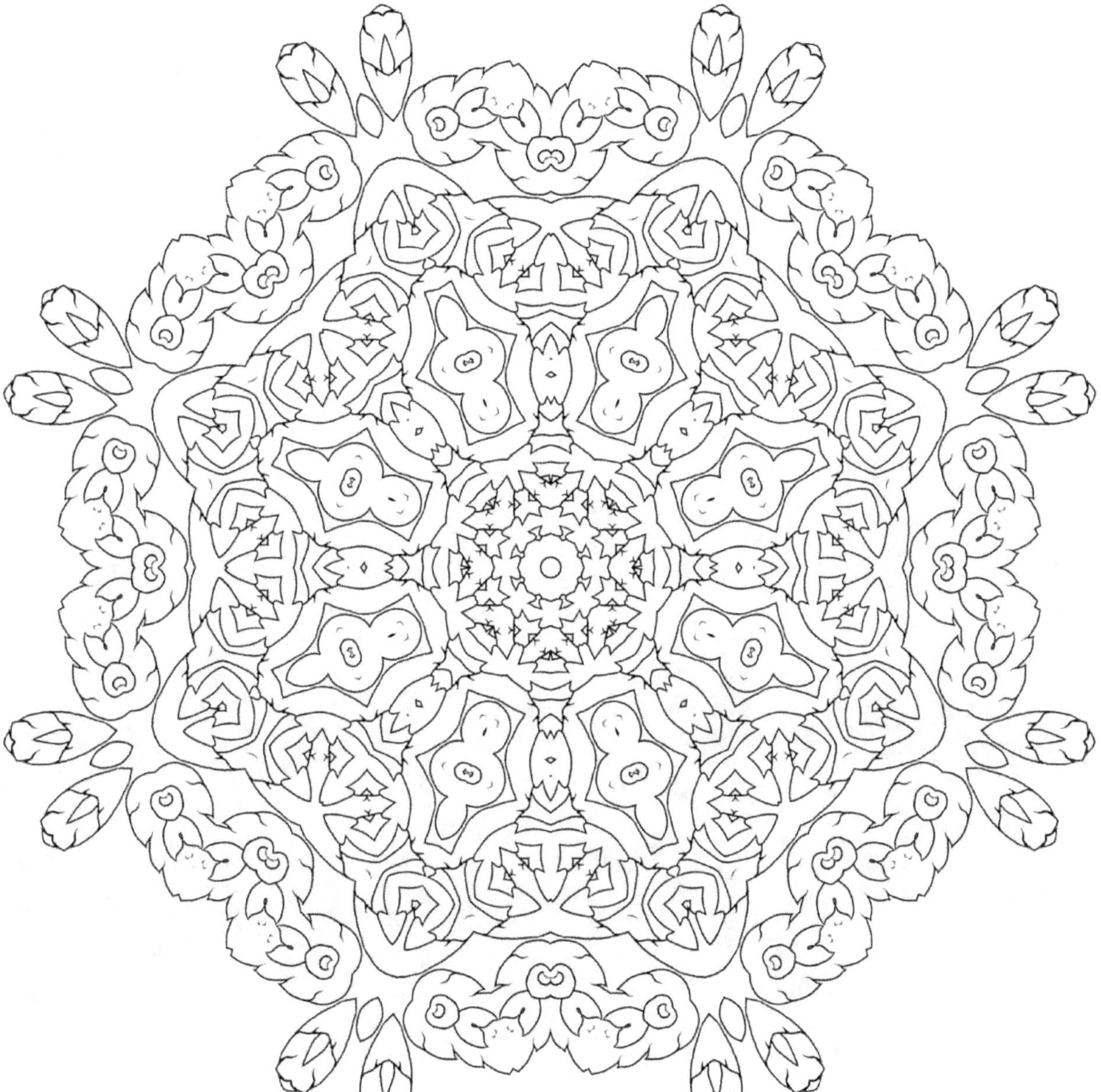

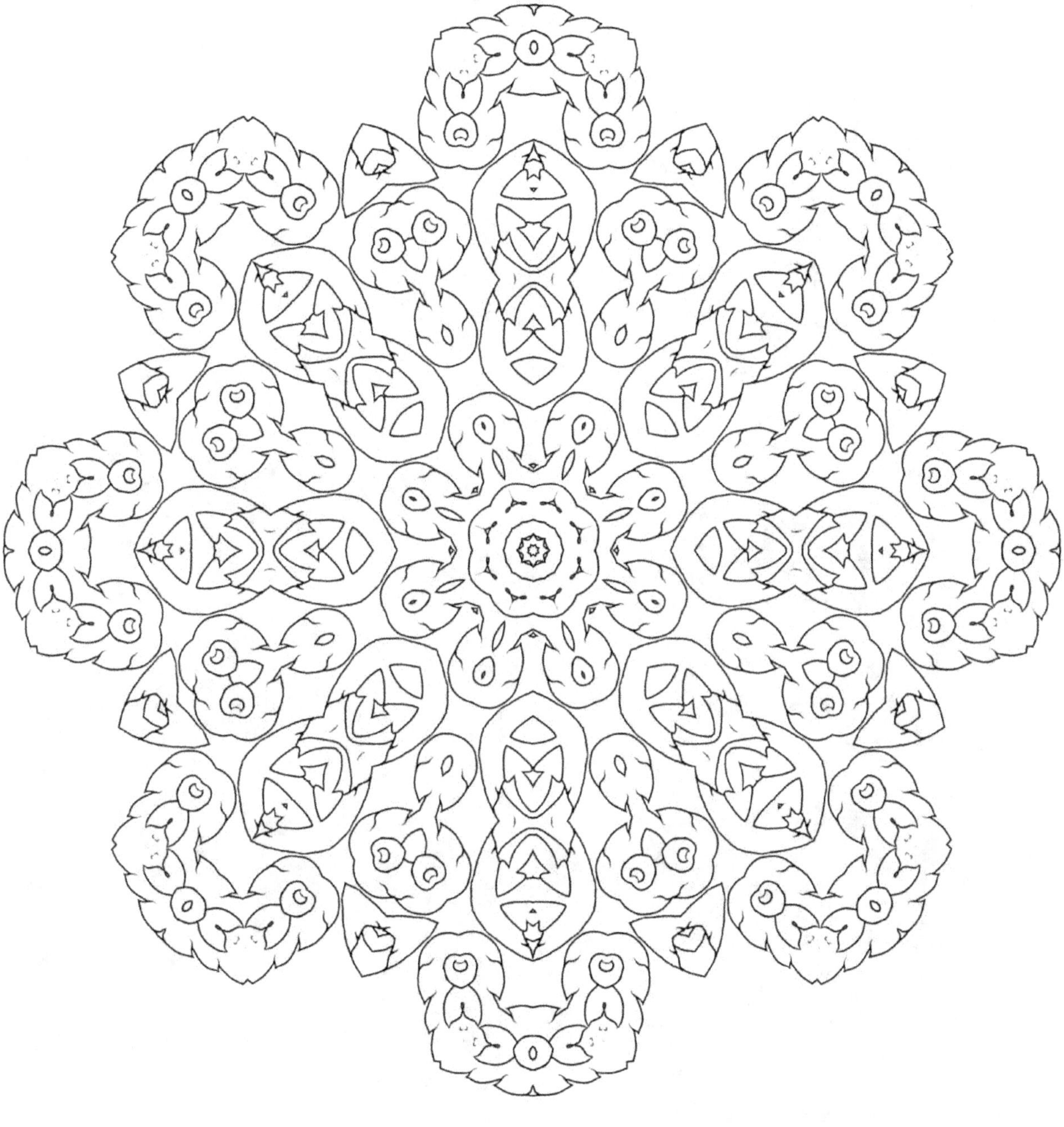

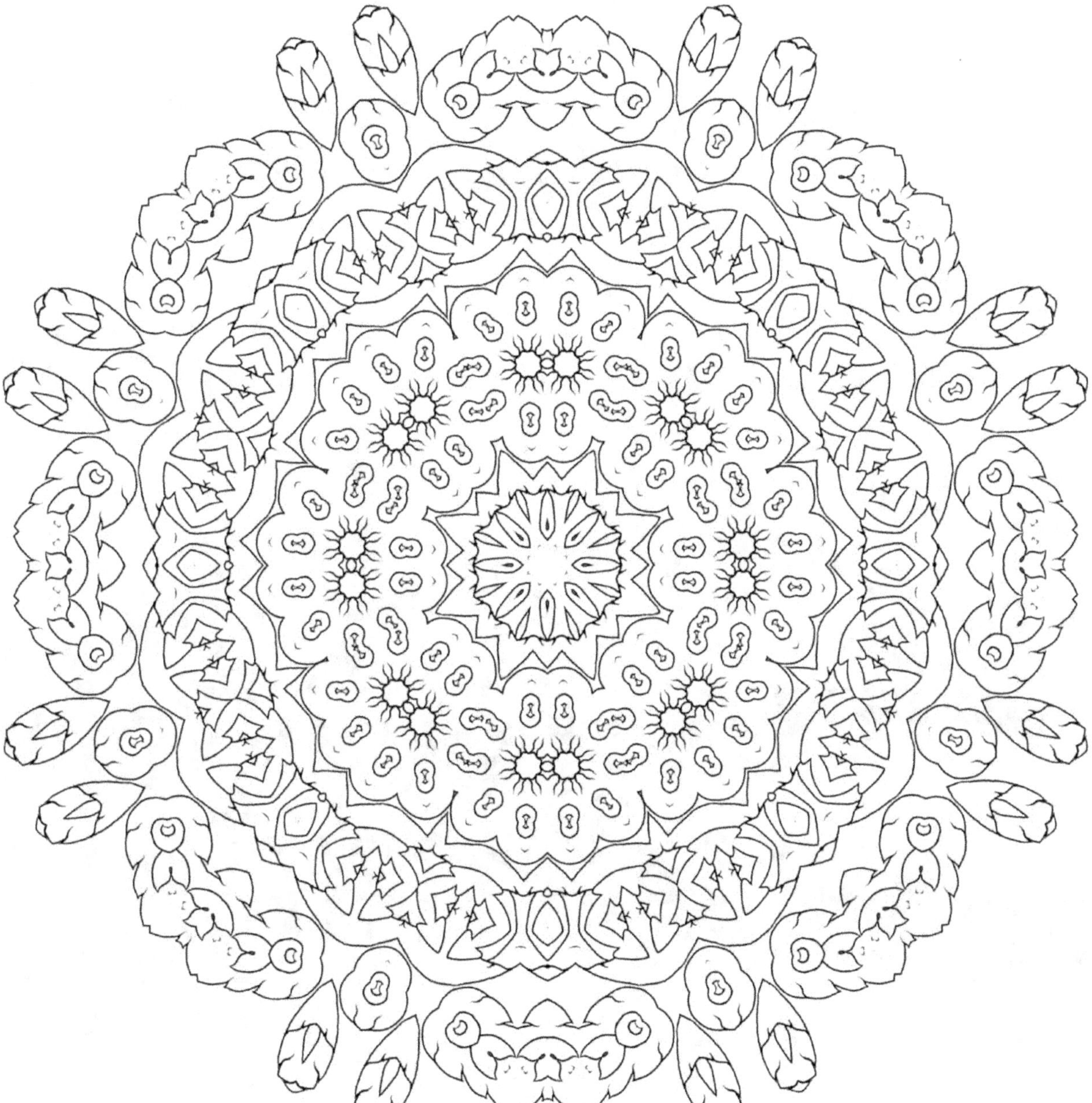

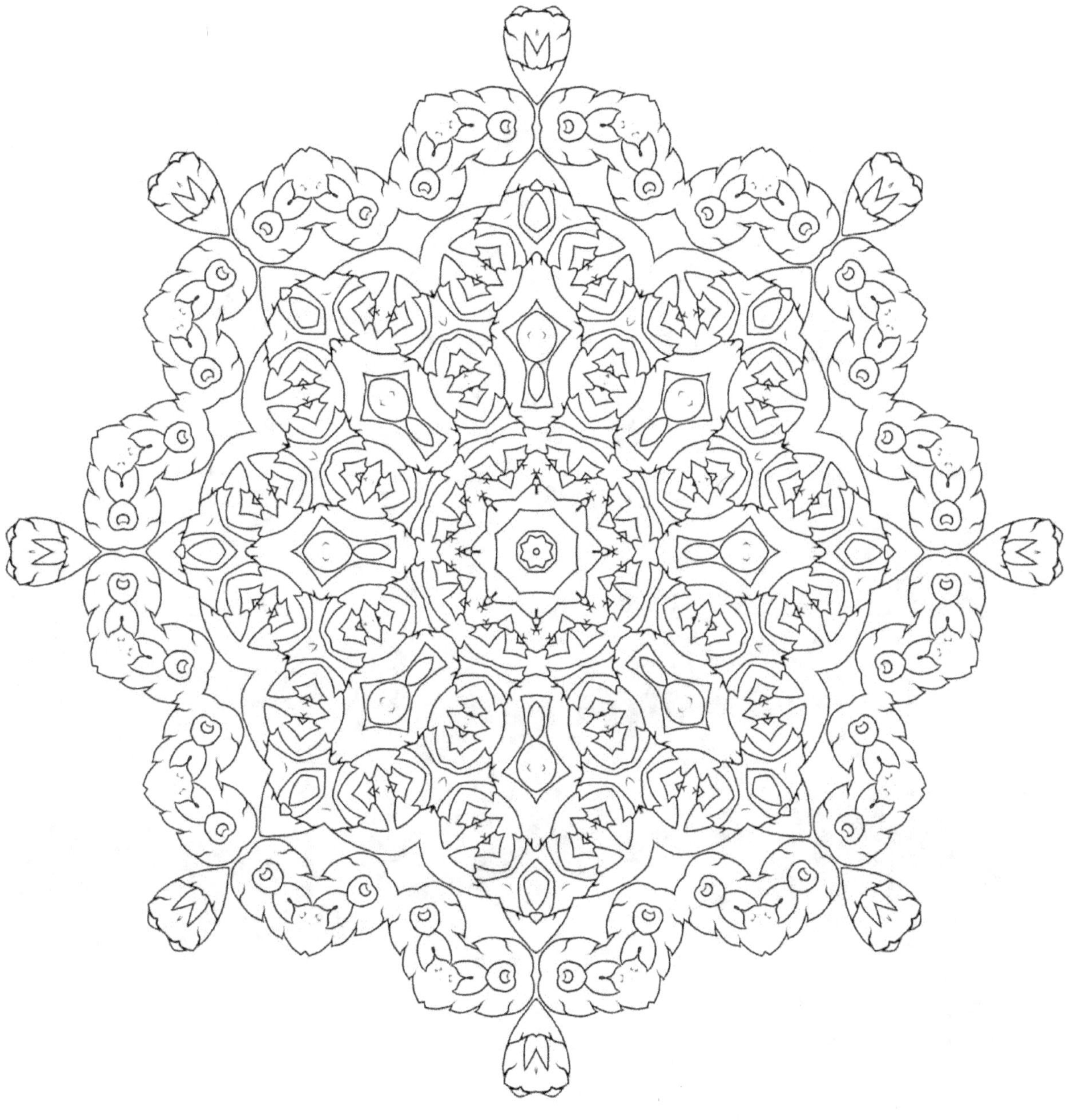

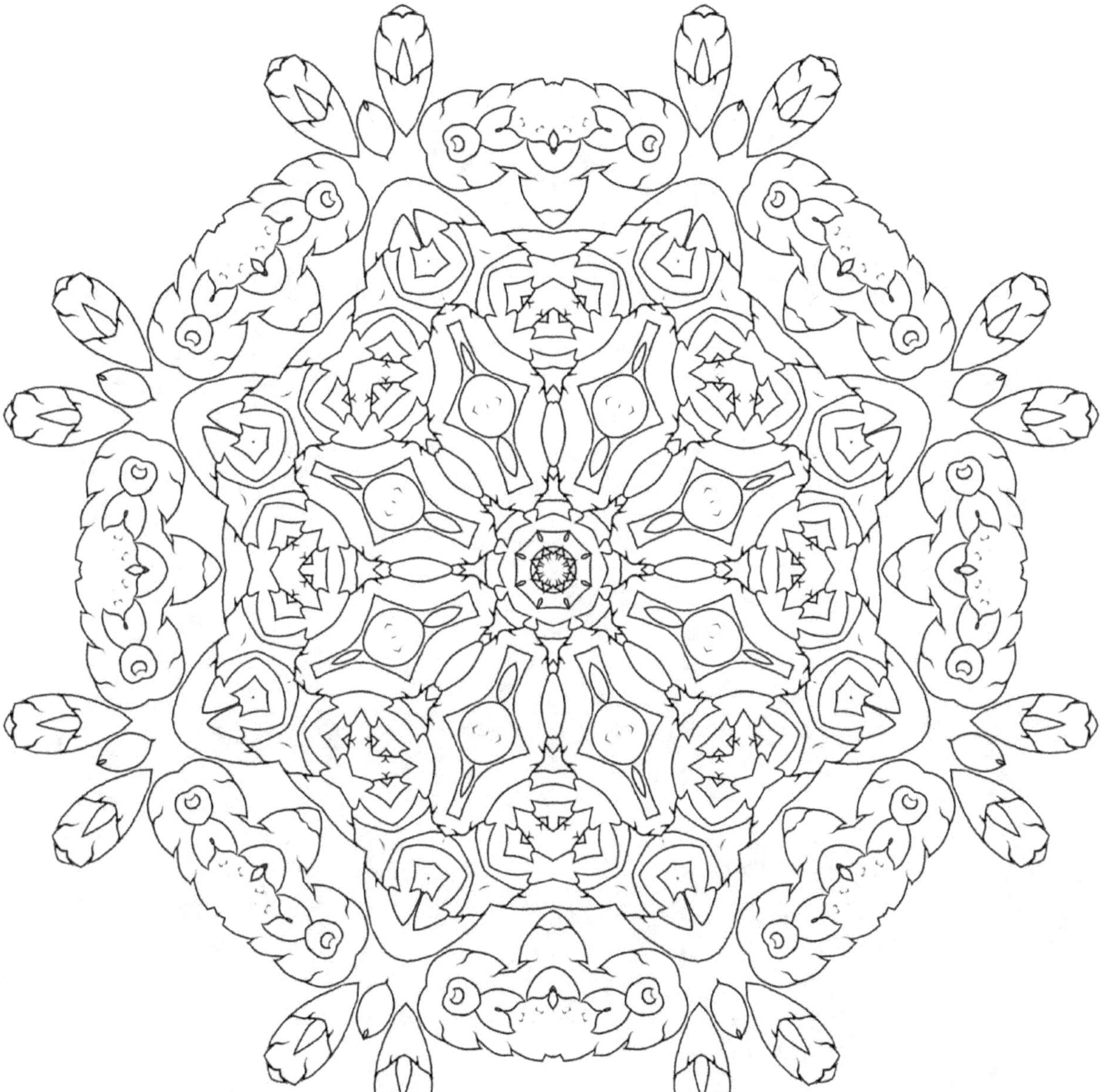

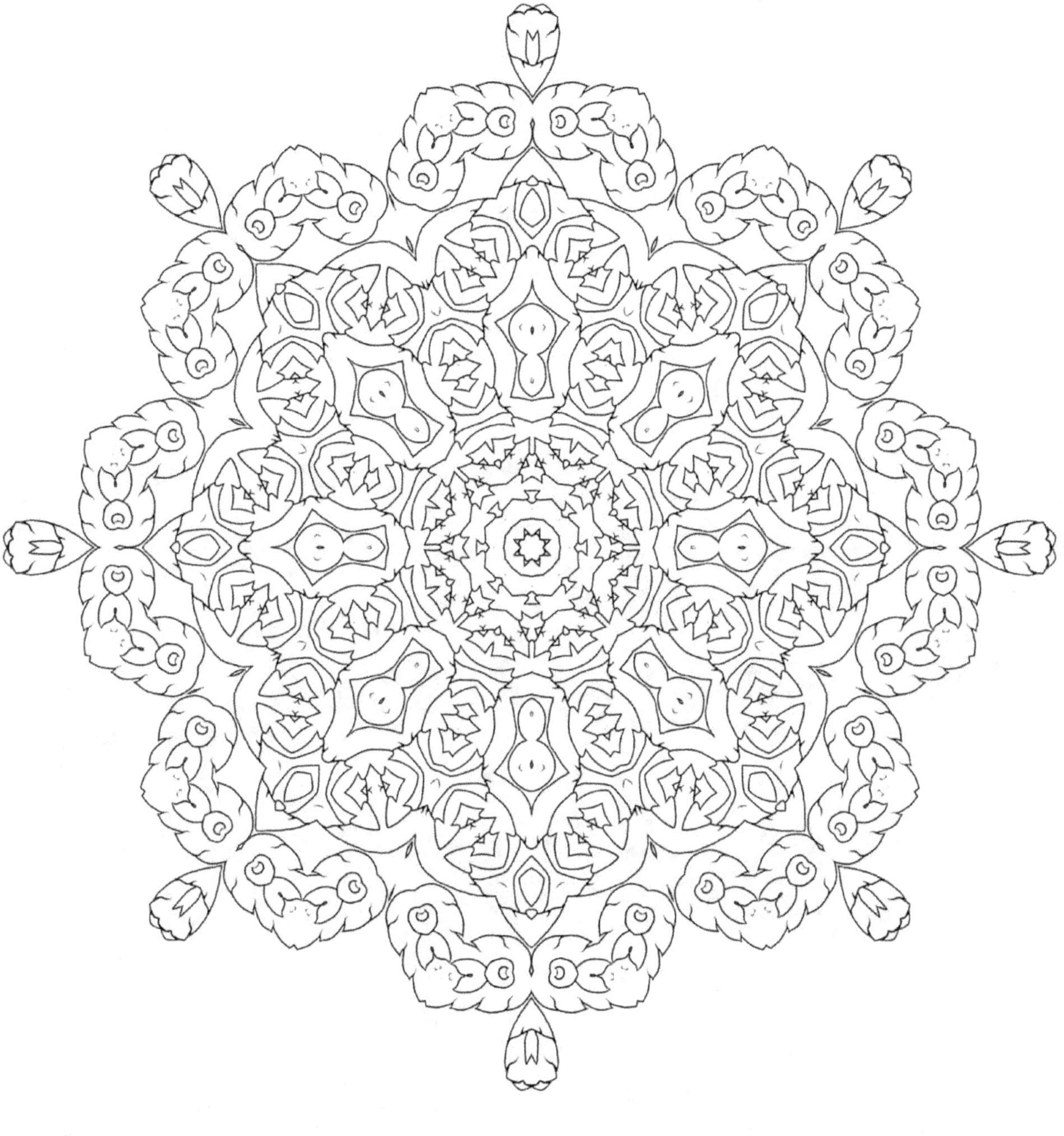

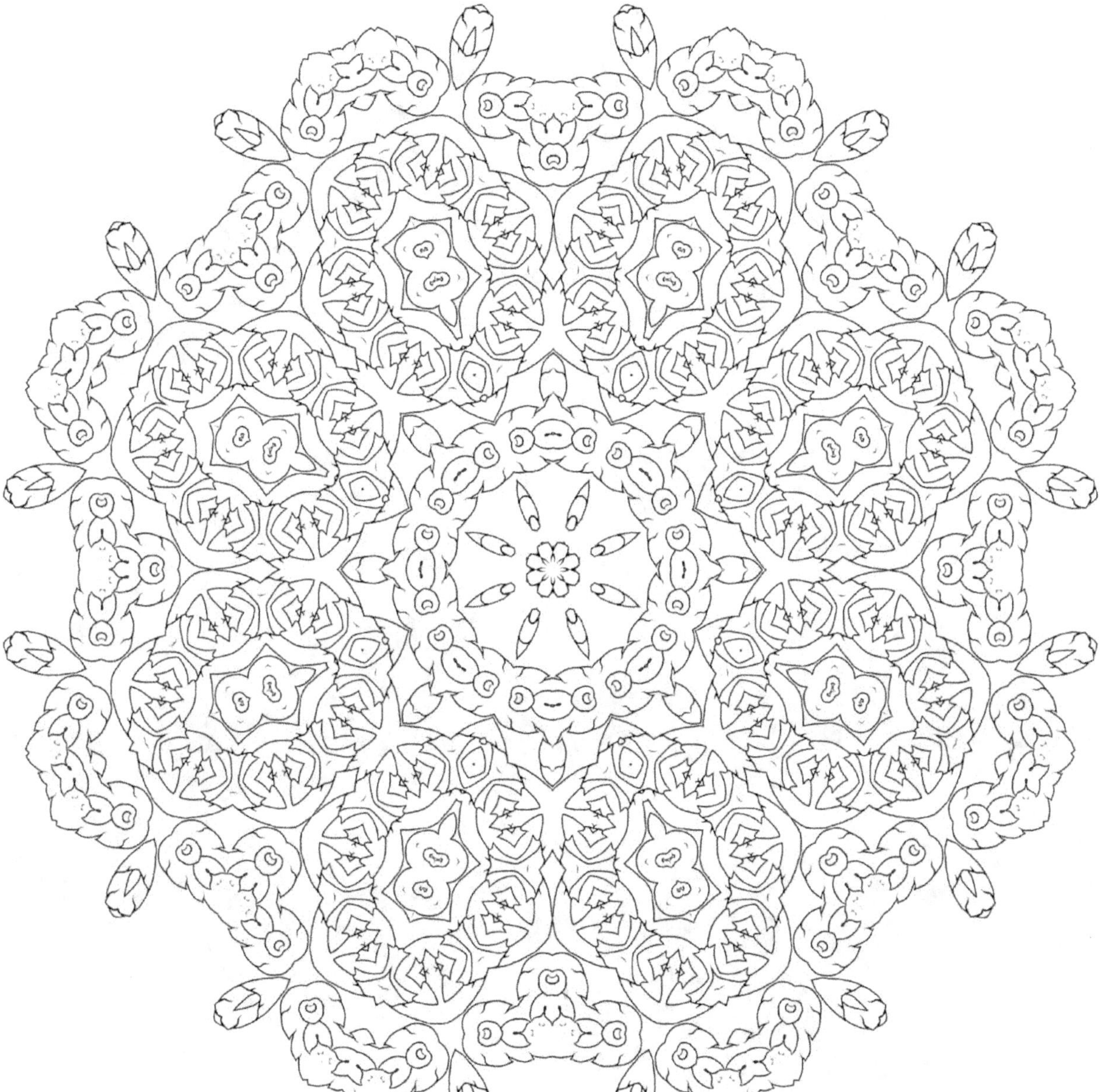

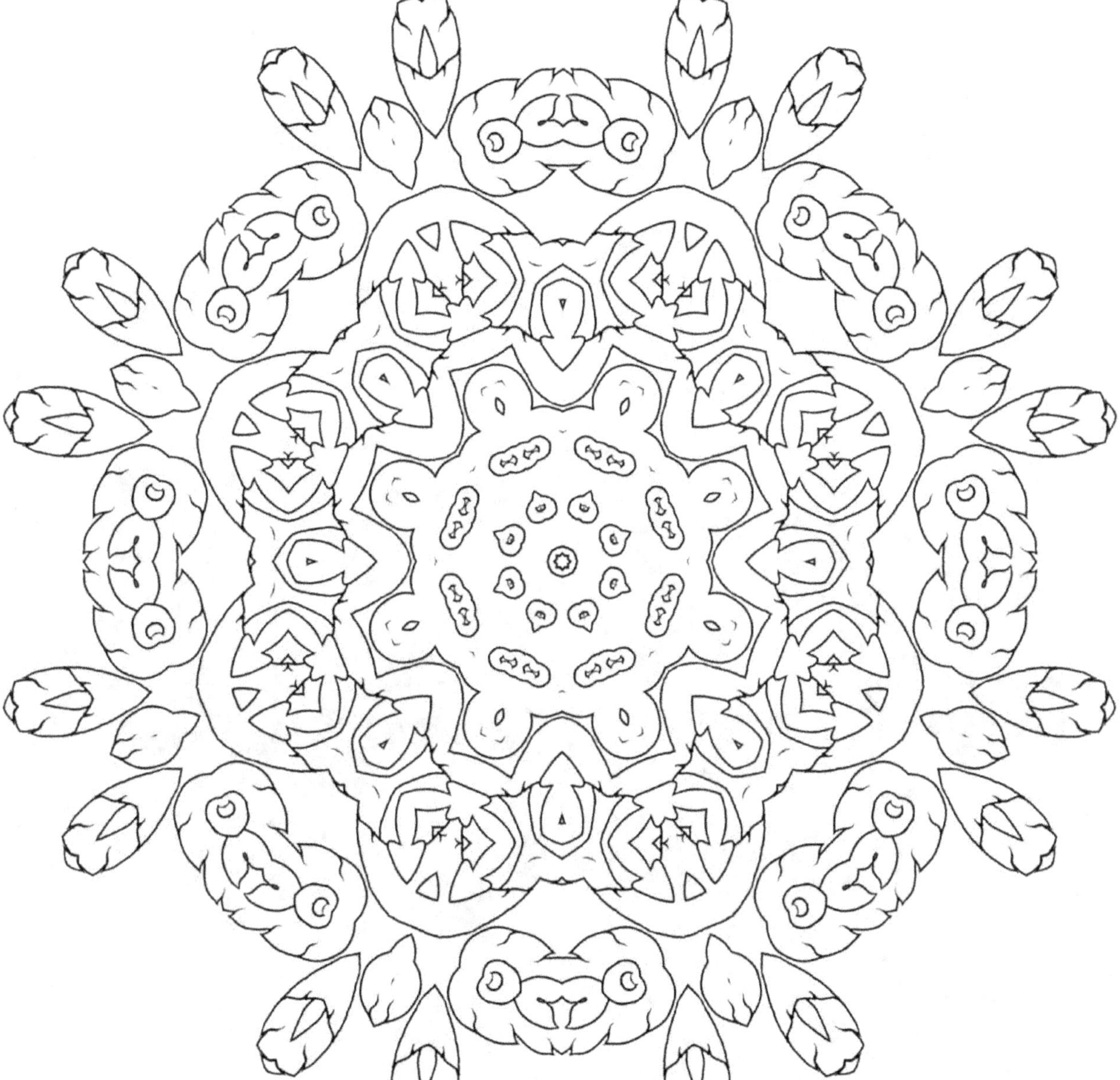

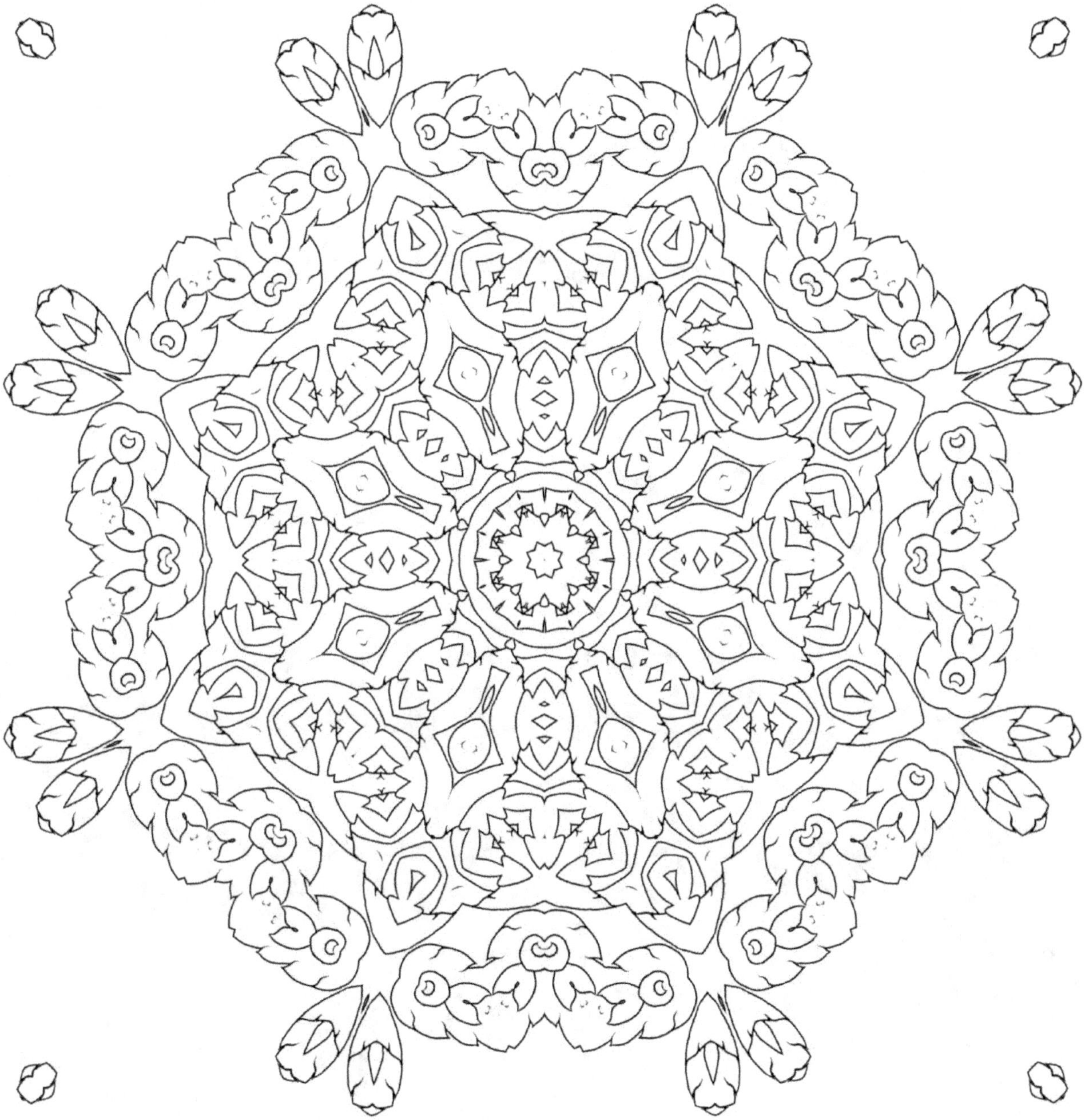

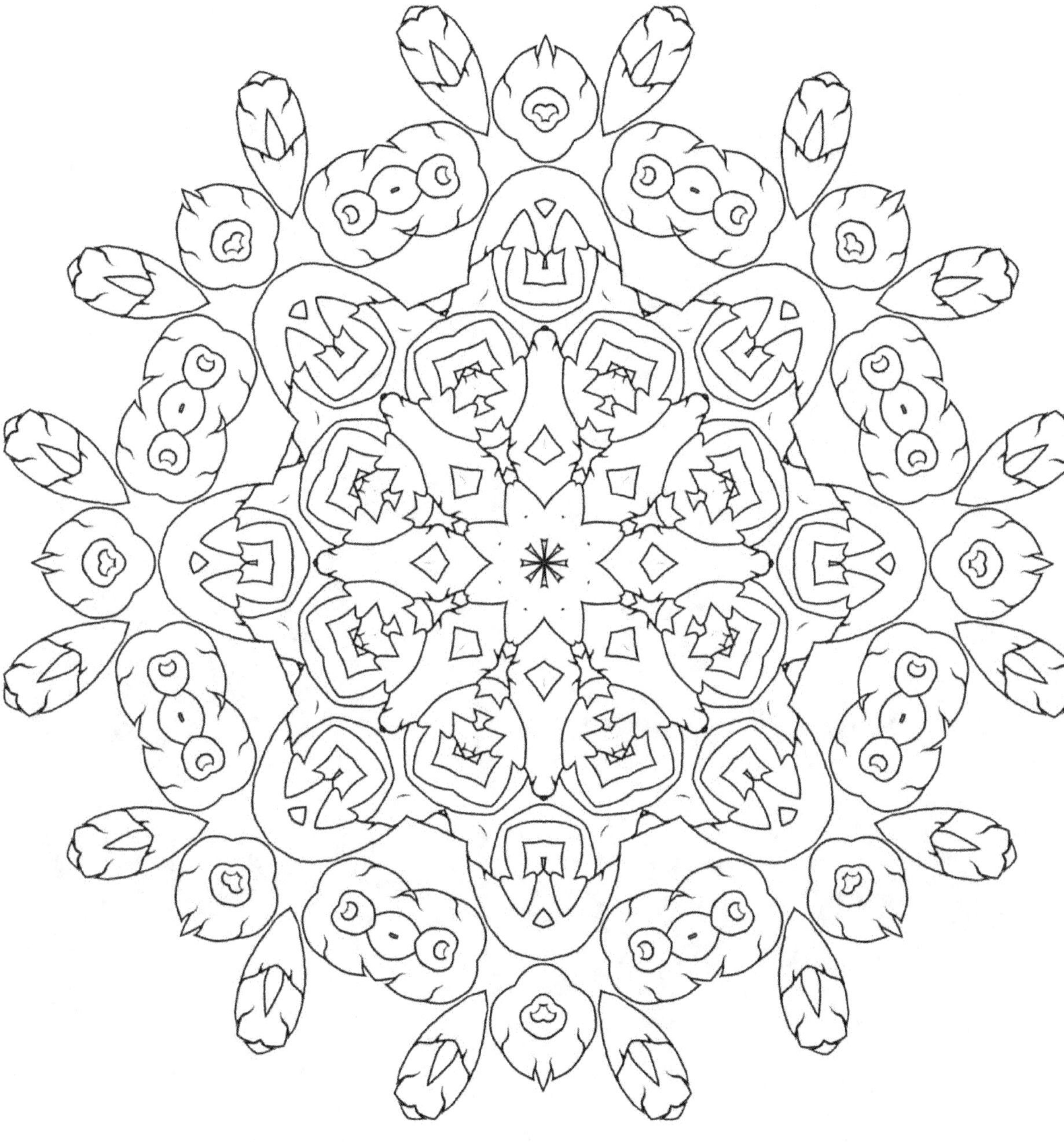

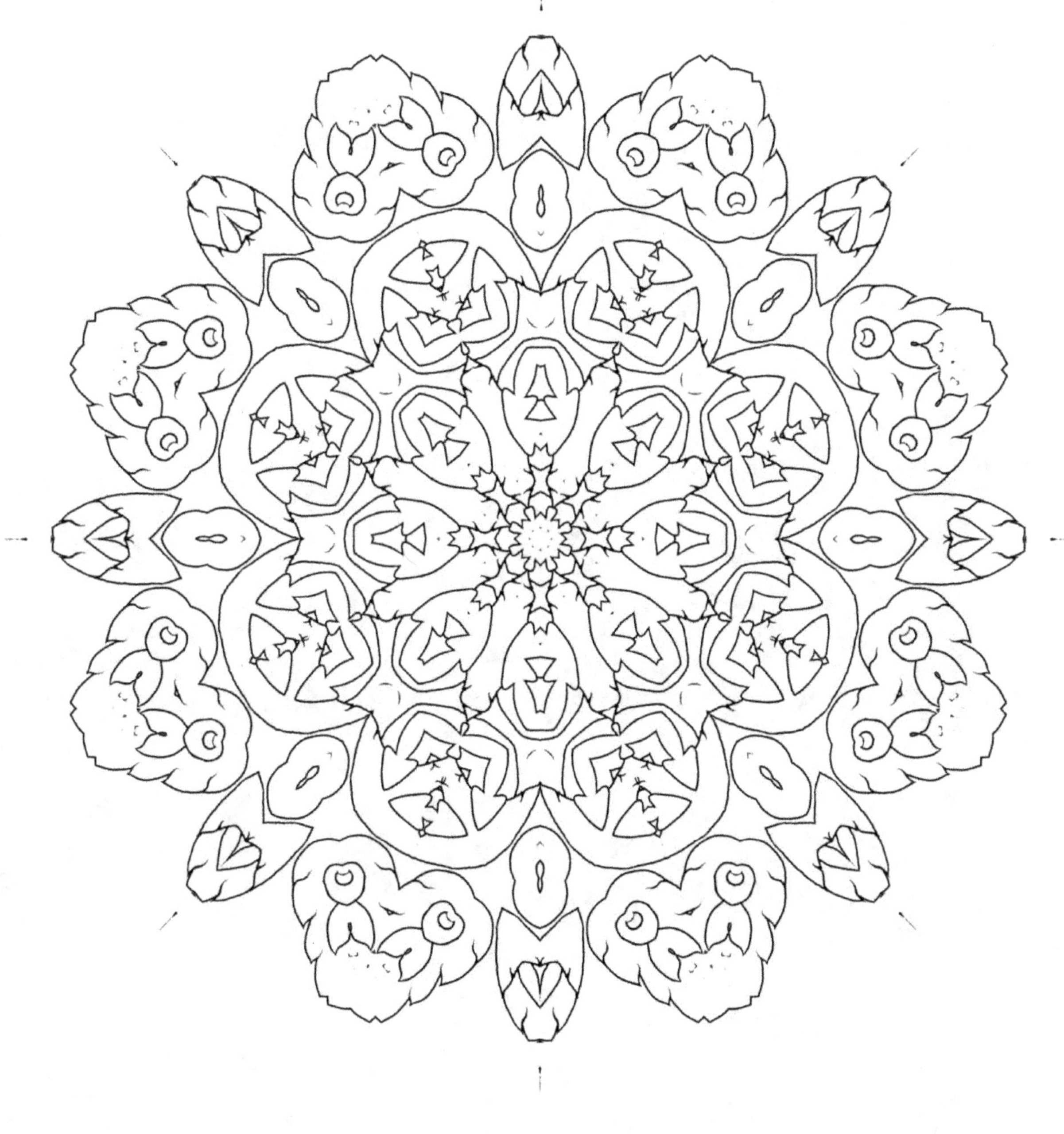

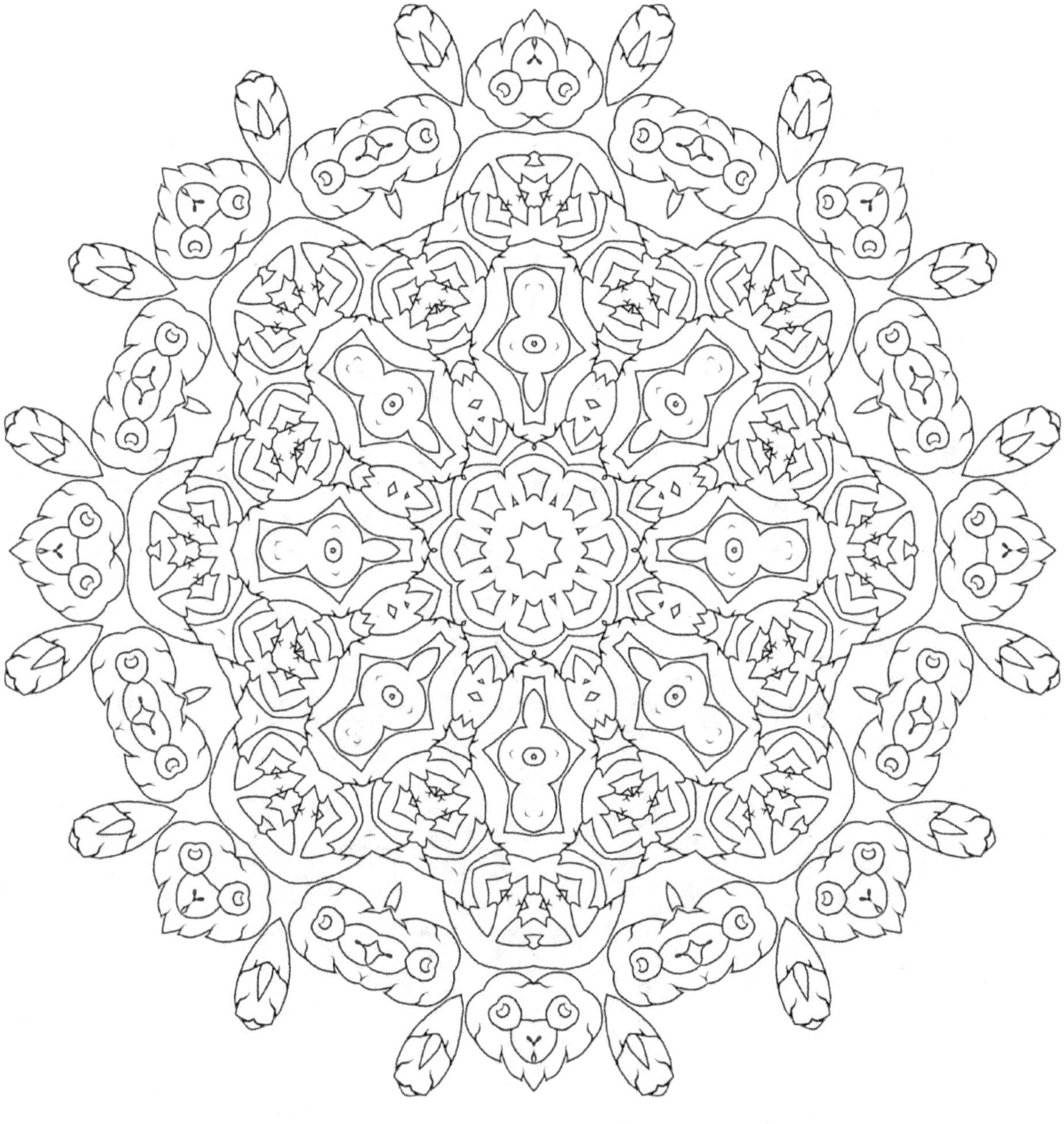

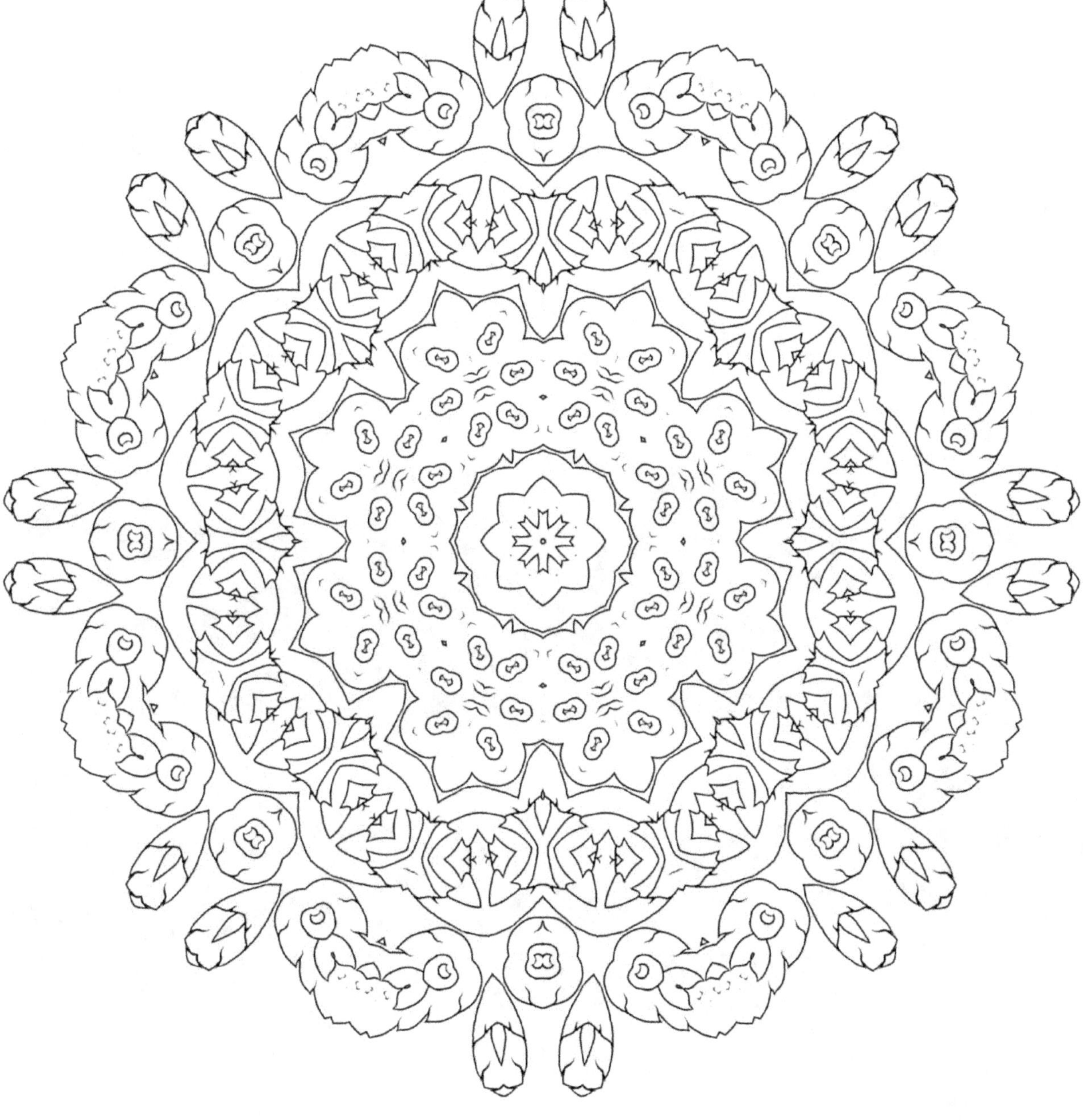

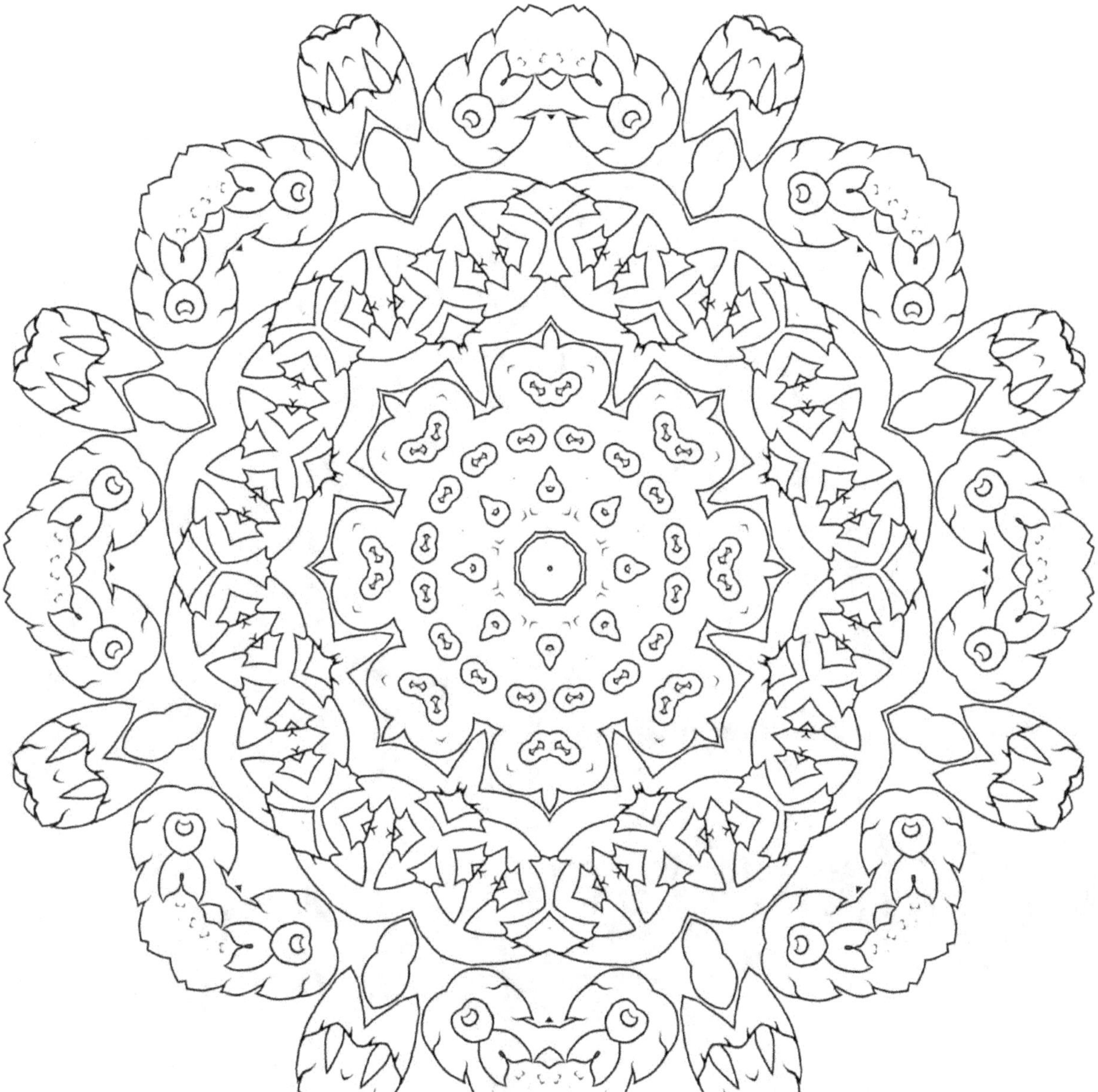

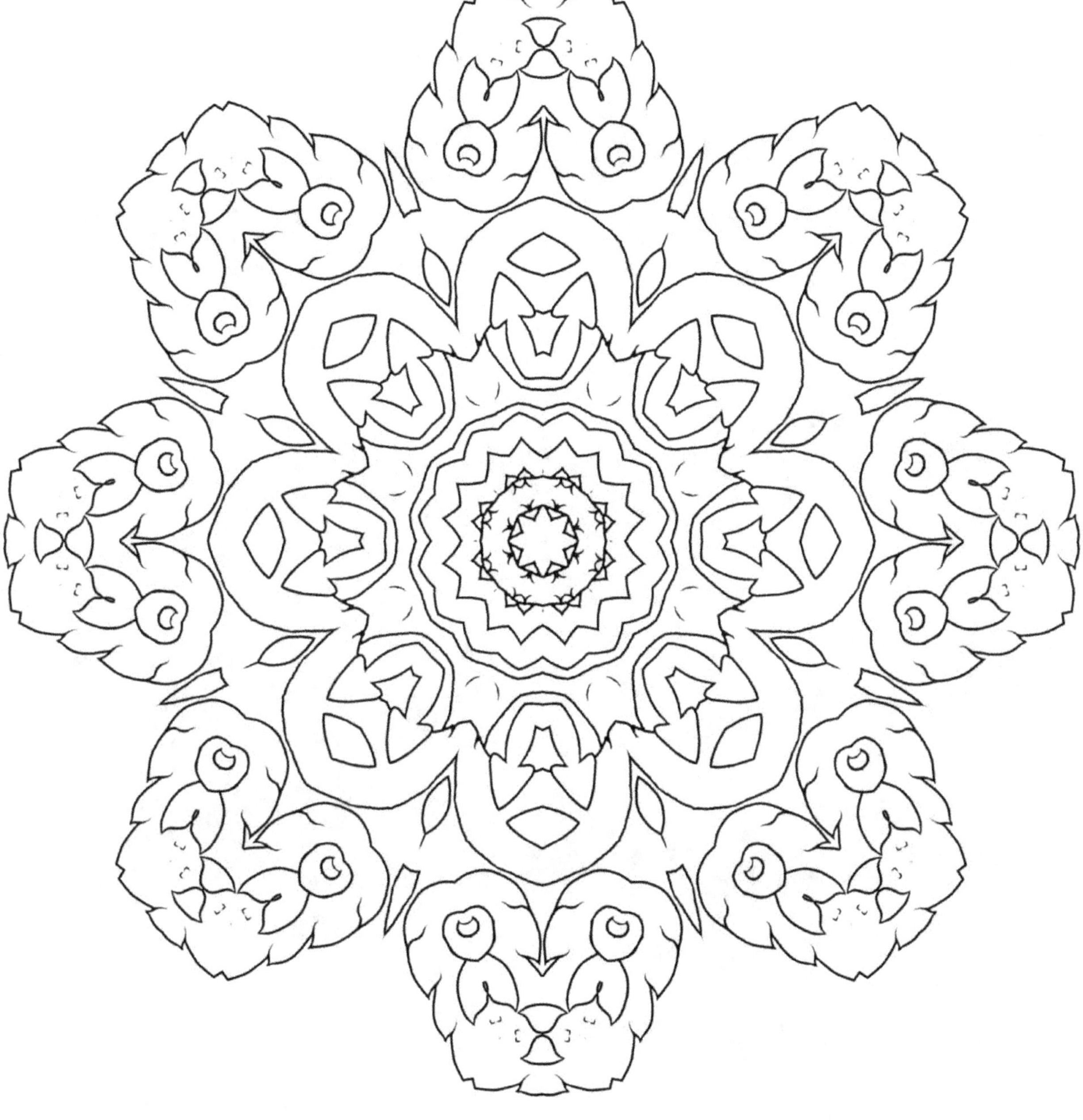

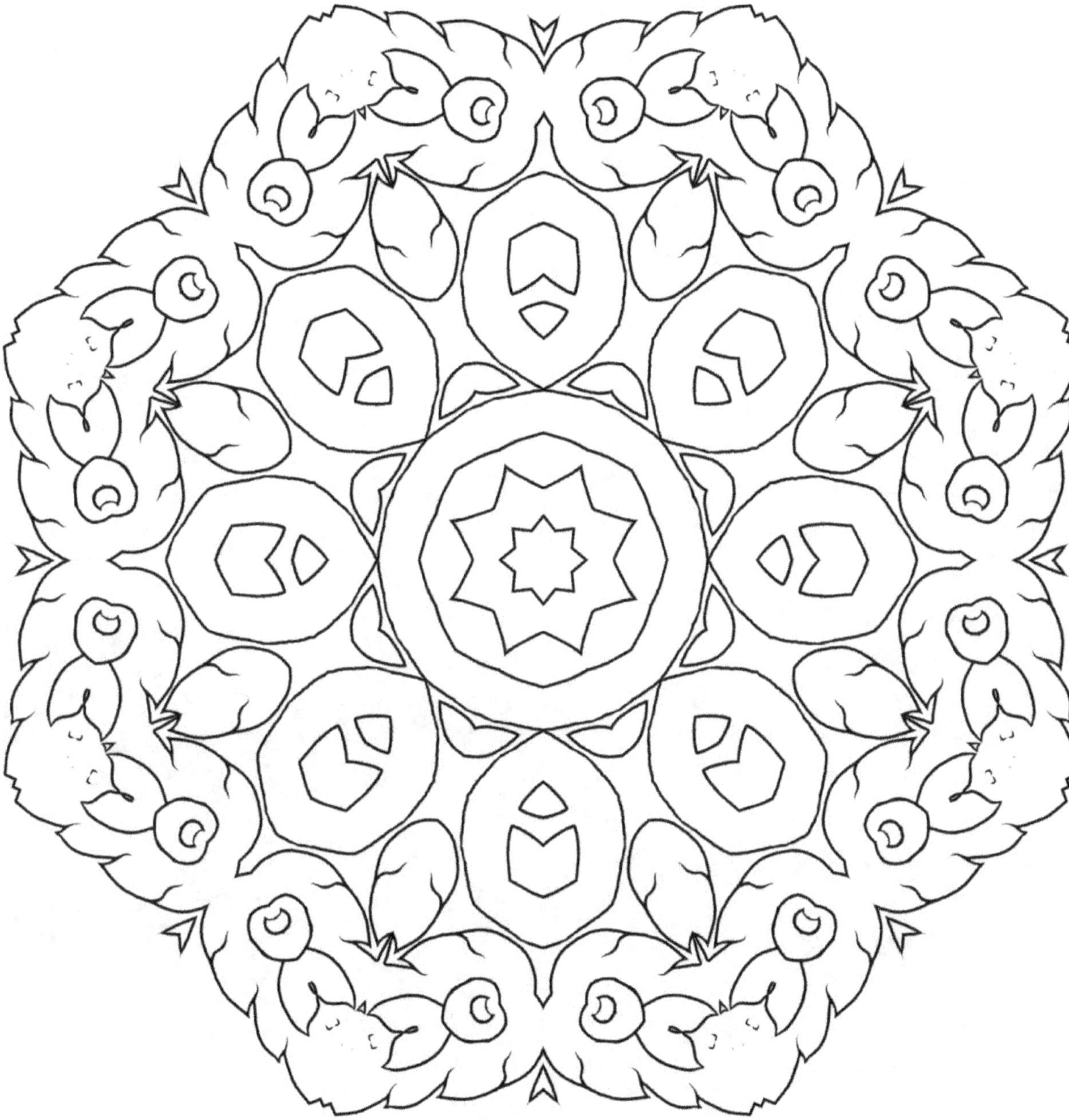

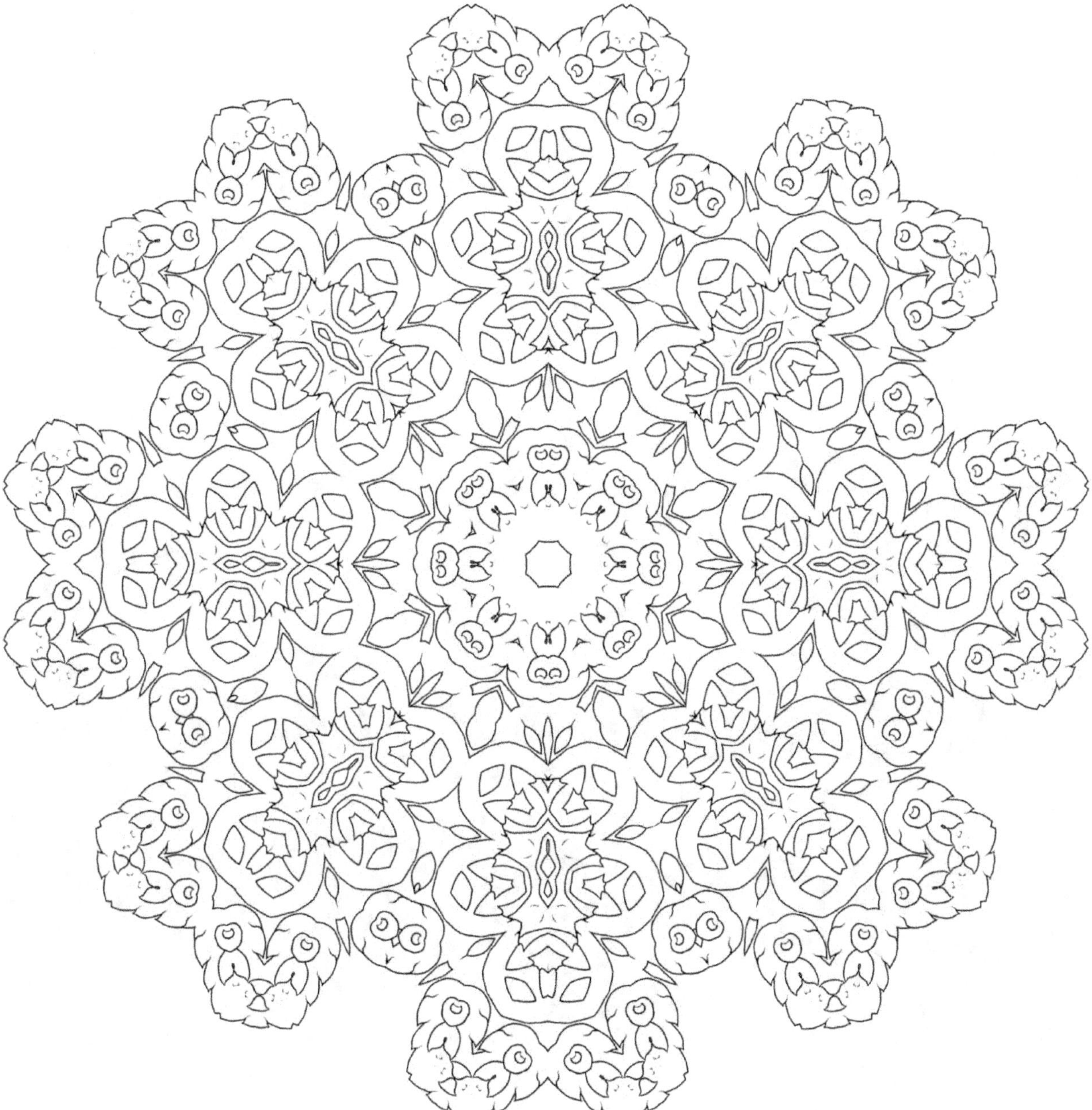

Thank you

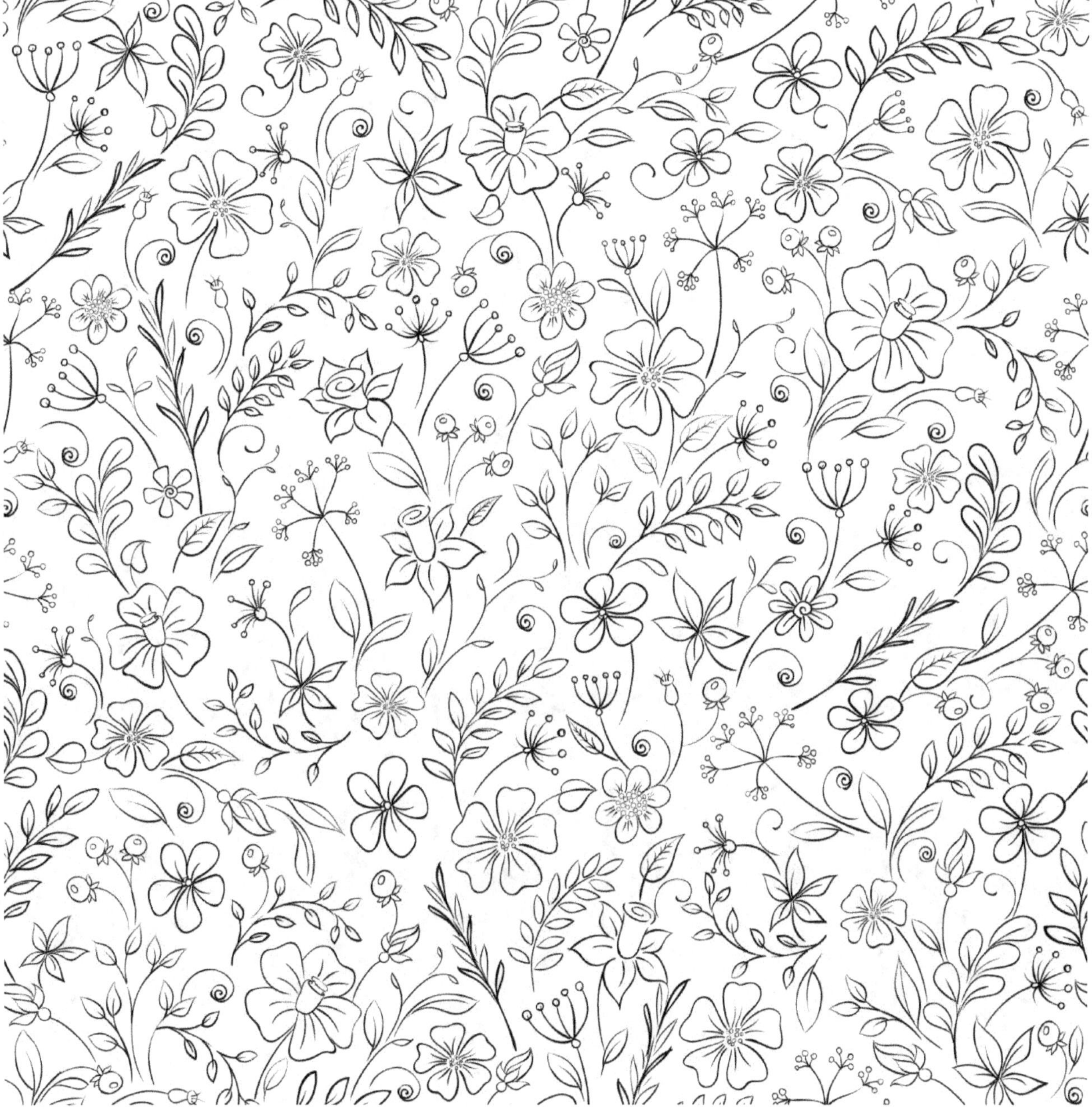

www.ingramcontent.com/pod-product-compliance
Lightning Source LLC
Chambersburg PA
CBHW082251220526
45469CB00009B/2959
* 9 7 8 1 7 2 4 8 6 9 7 5 3 *